Great Receivers Of The NFL

by Bill Gutman

tempo books

Grosset & Dunlap
Publishers • New York

ISBN: 0-448-12096-8
A Tempo Books Original
Tempo Books is registered in the U.S. Patent Office

Published simultaneously in Canada
Printed in the United States of America

Contents

Cliff Branch

It's a funny thing with world class sprinters, men who can zip off 100 yards in 9.2 or 9.3 seconds. They all think they can be football players, and thinking about best utilizing their speed, most of them decide that wide receiver is the spot.

But it doesn't usually work that way. The names of failed sprinters, even Olympic champions, are quite familiar. Frank Budd, Jim Hines, Tommie Smith, John Carlos—they are just some of the great speedsters who tried to make it in football as wide receivers. They didn't.

Of course, by now everyone is probably saying, "What about Bob Hayes?" Wasn't he an Olympic champion? And didn't he go on to become a great wide receiver with the Dallas Cowboys? True, he did. But there was a difference between Hayes and the others. Bob Hayes played football at Florida A & M and always considered himself a football player first and a sprinter second. And therein lies the secret.

Take Cliff Branch. He's classic, as far as football player-sprinters are concerned. As Cliff Branch made his way through the University of Colorado his stature as a world class sprinter grew. Records fell before his flying feet; he met and defeated many other well-known runners; there was talk about the 1972 Olympics and the great chance Cliff had of making the team.

But through it all, Cliff Branch maintained one thing, and maintained it steadfastly:

"Football is my game, and it's going to be my career. I enjoy running and enjoy track. But I've got to think of my future and that's why football will always have to come first."

So, like Bob Hayes before him, Cliff Branch was a football player first and a runner second. He never reached the same heights Hayes did as a sprinter, but Cliff Branch shows all indications of surpassing Hayes as a pass receiver.

It took a couple of years, but in 1974, Cliff Branch finally emerged. Playing for the powerhouse Oakland Raiders, Cliff grabbed 60 passes for 1,092 yards, an 18.2 average, and 13 big touchdowns. His yardage and TD totals were tops among all NFL receivers, and his clutch catches proved he was more than just a glorified speedboy. Cliff Branch has learned his craft well.

Cliff isn't a big guy, not even as wide receivers go. A receiver like Otis Taylor stands 6-3 and weighs some 215 pounds. Even Gene Washington of San Francisco, often thought of as a "little guy," goes 6-1, and about 190 pounds. But Branch is somewhere in the area of 5-10 (his height has been given as 5-9 to 5-11 on different occasions) and weighs in the neighborhood of 170-175 pounds. To be a top receiver at that size, speed notwithstanding, you've got to be tough and know what you're doing. Cliff Branch does.

Not that it all came easy. He was a burner at Colorado who set records returning kickoffs and punts. But he didn't make all-American as a receiver. One reason was the team didn't throw that much, and another was that Cliff just wasn't that classy, that experienced at the time. Yet when he joined the Raiders in 1972 he was impressive enough to win a starting job.

Then came game one. Cliff went out for a long bomb, was right there . . . and dropped it. Minutes later another rookie, Mike Siani, took his place. Though lacking Branch's speed, Siani was a battler who knew how to run patterns. He was impressive right from the start, and with all-pro veteran Fred Biletnikoff operating on the other side, Cliff sat the bench for the better part of two seasons.

He might still be sitting if Siani hadn't been injured early in 1974. That gave Cliff his chance.

And he made the most of it. He became an all-pro in his very first full year. Cliff Branch is here to stay.

Cliff was born in Houston, Texas, on August 1, 1948. He was never a big kid as a youngster and had to use his speed to compete with bigger, stronger boys. Fortunately, the speed was always there and pretty soon young Cliff realized what an advantage it was. It helped him in all the sports which he played with his friends.

Football and baseball were the natural sports the boys looked to, because they could always read about their heroes in the big leagues and the NFL. Track was different. It wasn't a glamor sport to the boys and very few of them participated in it until they reached school.

That was Cliff's story. But as soon as he reached Worthing High, the same all-black school attended earlier by Otis Taylor, his power as a sprinter was harnessed. Cliff quickly became a star, running the hundred, the two-twenty, and relays.

Branch was outstanding, make no mistake about that. On two occasions at Worthing High he tied the then world record of 9.3 in the 100-yard dash. That's running. It also meant at the time that on a given day he was capable of beating any sprinter in the world at that distance.

But being from a segregated high school in Texas, he didn't really get a wealth of publicity. College coaches didn't flock to see him or recruit him. Same with football. He was a receiver and kick return specialist, and a good one, though he had a lot to learn about running patterns and catching the football. But when he got up a head of steam returning a kickoff, he left everyone floundering in his wake. But, still, no big offers.

Even by then, Cliff knew it was football, and not track, that he wanted. "Pro ball had a hold on me, even then," he admits. "I didn't know if I'd be good enough, but there was more of a future in it than in track, though I enjoyed running, the competition, and winning."

With no real big offers to choose from, Cliff went to tiny Wharton County Junior College, not far from his home in Houston. He doubled as a football man and track man his freshman year, and received some feelers from the hometown University of Houston. He even practiced with their team for three days in the fall of 1968 before deciding to return to Wharton for another year.

Once back there, his athletic fortunes continued to rise. He was playing better football at end, and was already a first-class return specialist. And in track, he remained a burner of unlimited potential. Then, in the fall of 1969 he went big time. He enrolled at the University of Colorado.

"I went to Colorado because I liked the weather there," Cliff said. "Really. I didn't like the humidity in Houston even though I was raised there. I didn't know anyone at Colorado, either, but some of my friends knew people who really liked it up there. So I visited the place and I liked it, too."

Cliff was a junior when he entered Colorado and immediately joined the football team. One look at his blazing speed and the coaches knew they had a reservoir of unharnessed power on their hands. Cliff was immediately installed at wide receiver and made the team's top kickoff return man. Then he started showing his stuff.

Every time he camped under a punt or kickoff the fans moved to the edge of their seats. And he didn't disappoint. Five times during the 1970 season he hauled kicks back all the way for touchdowns. He was Mr. Excitement to the Colorado fans, and to all fans who saw him play.

His potential as a receiver was also showing. During his first year at Colorado, Cliff hauled in 23 passes for 335 yards, yet his inexperience showed up here. He didn't take a single pass in for a score.

"I would practice and practice running patterns," Cliff recalls, "but in the games I just didn't have much of a chance to catch the football. That hurt me later, because I didn't have the same kind of experience as players from teams that threw the ball more often."

In the spring, Cliff was on the track team, and he lost football time at spring practice. But it was worth it to the Colorado cindermen. Cliff was one of the stars from the start. In fact, he joined several other top runners at a new 100-yard standard of 9.2. Some thought he still had the potential to be one of the world's best. Talk was already starting about the Olympics of 1972, and Cliff was mentioned as a prime candidate in the sprints. It was an immediate problem since a try for the Olympics and inclusion on the team could mean being away from football in what could be Cliff's rookie year in the NFL.

"It was too early for a concrete decision since it was still more than a year away," Cliff said. "But I didn't want to blow a chance to make it in the pros. At the same time, it's quite an honor to represent your country at the Olympics. So during my junior year I kind of left the books open on that one."

Cliff was thinking all football when he returned for his senior year of 1971. It was both successful and disappointing for him. His success came as a return man. Cliff was simply tremendous.

On eight occasions he returned kicks all the way to the end zone for touchdowns, six of them coming on punts. And he had three TD's called back because of clipping penalties. These figures were NCAA records.

The disappointing part of it was his pass receptions. The team threw even fewer passes than the year before, with Cliff grabbing just 13 of them. But this time he gained 330 yards, an average of more than 25 yards a catch, showing his ability as a deep receiver for the first time. He also scored three times via receptions in '71. That gave Cliff 16 touchdowns during his two-year career at Colorado.

Toward the end of the season Cliff began getting some feelers from pro teams.

"I really want to play pro ball," he told a reporter. "Right now I'd like nothing better than to get a chance with the Denver Broncos so I could be with Bobby Anderson again." Anderson had been the Colorado quarterback during Cliff's junior year.

But there was a question about Cliff's ability, one that seems to afflict most sprinters who want to play pro. The word was that he had bad hands.

Cliff split playing time with a receiver named Willie Nichols that year. Nichols, though by no means fast, had a great set of hands and caught anything he could reach. The standard gag in Colorado football circles was that a combination of Branch's speed and Nichols' hands would add up to an all-pro player. Cliff took the rap with his usual good nature, but in serious moments blamed it on the fact that he just hadn't had the chance to catch enough passes in game conditions. In other words, he still lacked a great deal of experience.

Colorado was good in 1971, as indicated by wins against LSU and Ohio State, two powerhouse teams. Those games came early in the season and Cliff ran wild on kick returns. Later, opposing teams got smart and began kicking away from the speed merchant.

"They started kicking squibblers right after midseason," he said. "And on punts the kickers were always trying to angle the ball out of bounds."

But for the most part it was a satisfying senior year. The club even accepted a bowl bid to the Astro-Bluebonnet Bowl in Houston, where Cliff got a chance to end his career in front of the hometown fans.

By then most area fans knew all about Cliff. In fact, the Colorado publicity department billed him as "America's fastest football player," and few people felt like arguing with that description. In fact, once the football season ended he got ready for another season of track, one that could be very crucial to his future.

Cliff played in one all-star game that year, the Hula Bowl in Honolulu, Hawaii. Then he hit the cinders. A week after that game he ran a six-second 60-yard dash in Albuquerque, and two weeks after that equaled the world record in the event with a 5.9 clocking. He was still world class. Track people marveled at the way he jumped from the bruising contact of football to the delicate balance of sprinting. Cliff said it was easy.

"Nothing to it as long as I'm in shape. There really isn't much difference in the conditioning."

But shortly after the winter track circuit began, Cliff learned something else. He was the number four draft pick of the Oakland Raiders, one of the best teams in all of pro football. It was good news, all right, the thing he had always wanted.

Cliff had just purchased a new puppy when he

was drafted. He promptly named the canine "Raider." "Now that I'm going to be an Oakland Raider in professional football, I couldn't name him anything else, could I?"

He sounded like a man who couldn't wait to put on that pro uniform. But it wasn't that simple, for in the next breath, Cliff Branch was saying:

"I don't intend to sign any pro contract until after our track season ends. Then I'll wait and see how I've done in the outdoor meets and how I feel before thinking seriously about the Olympic trials."

So there was still a conflict. Track and the Olympics were amateur sports. If Cliff signed any kind of pro pact with the Raiders, he would have to end his track career right then and there.

Cliff was caught in a kind of bind, all right. He kept telling people how happy he was to be picked by the Raiders because the team was so competitive and had a winning tradition. He had a few regrets about not being picked by the Broncos because he loved the state of Colorado and the people, saying that he intended to make his permanent home there. Football kept sounding like number one.

Then someone reminded him that Bobby Hayes had gotten a better contract from Dallas in 1964 after winning the 100-meter run in the Olympics. Cliff agreed, "Yes, I probably would be in a better position for a good bonus."

So it became of question of just what the youngster would do. It wasn't an easy decision for him because the timing was bad. The 1972 NCAA track championships were scheduled for the beginning of June. Then at the beginning of July the Olympic trials would begin. Right away it would be cutting into his first pro training camp. The Olympics were several months after that, so if by chance Cliff made the team and went to Munich, Germany, he'd be missing the entire training camp and possibly part of the season. Then he'd have to get in shape for football all over again. Conceivably, the whole season could be down the drain by then. By contrast, the thrill of competing in the Olympics usually comes just once in a lifetime.

By mid-May Cliff was concentrating on track, but reporters didn't let him forget about football. The same questions were always there, and Cliff's answer always about the same.

"I've always loved the sport of track and always thought about going to the Olympics. But on the other hand I've always wanted to play pro football and right now that's still number one with me."

One man who wasn't thinking football was Cliff's track coach at Colorado, Don Meyers. He talked about the intricacies of the sprints and about how he was preparing Cliff for an assault on the Olympics.

"Last year Cliff peaked out too soon," the coach said. "He ran a 9.2 early in the year and thought it was going to be gravy. But I remember before the NCAA title meet Cliff said he felt tight and in the meet itself he had nothing.

"This year we have worked very hard early and have tried to prevent Cliff from getting high too soon with the idea that by the time June comes he will have a better chance of giving his best performance.

"Cliff is very fast off the mark, but is not as consistent out of the blocks as he might be. And when you're not consistent you can get whipped."

Coach Meyers sounded as if he were prepping his runner for a big season. The question was just how far Cliff was willing to go. The Raiders had already been in contact with him and indicated in a backhanded kind of way that they didn't want him trying for the Olympics, which wouldn't be held until the end of August.

In one breath Cliff said, "If I'm running well by the trials, I'll go." But in the next breath—"The Raiders said they want to use me as a wide receiver and for kickoff and punt returns this year. They said they're not thinking in terms of next year."

Obviously this dilemma was on Cliff's mind as the big meets approached. It's hard to say whether or not it affected his performance, but there was certainly an implication that the Olympics could cost him the start of his football career, or perhaps his entire chance at football.

The situation was resolved at the NCAA title meet. Cliff ran a snappy 10 seconds flat in the 100 meter semi-final, then slipped to 10.1 in the finals. It was a close race, in which the first five finishers all were timed in 10.1. Unfortunately, the fifth-place man was Cliff Branch. That did it. There'd be no Olympic trials and no Olympics. But Cliff wasn't dismayed.

"I never intended to try for the Olympics," he said, later. "I've wanted to be a pro football player since high school and there was too much to lose if I went to the Olympics."

True to his word, Cliff immediately contacted Raiders officials and with no hassle whatsoever, signed a contract for his rookie year. At last he was at peace.

Of course, there was now pressure of another kind. He had to make the team and try to win himself a starting spot. So he worked hard right from the start. According to his new coach, John Madden, he needed all the work he could get.

"Cliff is working hard because he has to," said Madden. "He has a lot of catching up to do. Being a track man of his caliber demonstrates he can run fast, but it also tells you that he missed a lot of practice time.

"Everyone else had a month or six weeks of spring football for three years. Cliff didn't. Missing those spring practices for track can add up."

Longtime Raider quarterback Daryle Lamonica liked Cliff, comparing his style with the other rookie receiver, Mike Siani.

"Cliff is as good looking a rookie as I've seen,"

said Lamonica. "His speed impresses you, of course, but he's getting there with moves, too. He has good body control to go with his speed.

"Mike Siani impressed me as being smooth to read, a well-polished rookie receiver."

The Raider game plan read like this. Branch would be the speed receiver and probably back up the explosive Warren Wells, while Siani would be the move receiver, playing behind the crafty Fred Biletnikoff. But it didn't work out that way, simply because Wells ran into personal problems and wouldn't be back. Now there was a wide receiver slot up for grabs, with Cliff and Siani the prime candidates.

Cliff continued to work hard and look good. He ran the short and medium patterns well, and when he went deep, his speed amazed everyone.

"World class speed comes in handy on the deep ones," he said. "It's nice to be able to count on that extra step, but there's a lot more to receiving than that. Fred Biletnikoff, for example, doesn't have sprinter's speed, but he can beat every defensive back in the league. He's always open. He's got good body control and great hands, and that's what I'm working to achieve."

Apparently, Cliff achieved enough to impress the coaches. He had a pretty good pre-season, but so did Siani. It must have been his speed that gave him the edge, because shortly before the 1972 opener against Pittsburgh, Cliff was named a starter opposite Fred Biletnikoff.

Starting for the Oakland Raiders was no small task. The franchise was among the most successful in football, and though the club had not yet reached the ultimate—the Super Bowl—its won-lost record since 1963 was the best in all of pro ball. From 1967 to 1969, the club had regular-season marks of 13–1, 12–2, and 12–1–1. That's 37–4–3 for three seasons. Yet the club reached the Super Bowl just once, losing to Green Bay in the second super game ever played.

Still, the team kept up its high quality, even while rebuilding from within. In 1971, the club slipped slightly to 8–4–2, losing the divisional title to Kansas City. Now, in 1972, they wanted it back.

So Cliff was in the starting lineup as the club took the field at Pittsburgh. It was to be a wide open game, with plenty of passing on both sides. It looked like the young receiver would get his chance to show early. He did.

It was a deep pattern, the kind of bomb Cliff was supposed to catch. He raced downfield past the Pittsburgh defender as quarterback Lamonica uncorked. The ball arched high and deep and into Cliff's hands . . . then right out again!

"I was clear for the touchdown," Cliff said. "Wide open. But the defensive back came over and swiped at the ball. He missed it, but his arm must have distracted me, because I missed it, too. It went right through my hands."

If it hadn't been an important and close game between two power teams, the coaches might have stuck with Cliff. But at the beginning of the second half Siani was given a crack at the job. And as they say, he made the most of the opportunity.

Minutes after entering the game, the young receiver was on the end of a 70-yard bomb from Lamonica. Touchdown. Cliff watched from the bench as the Raiders mobbed Siani, who had done what he (Cliff) was supposed to do. And it wasn't a fluke. Before the game was over Siani had grabbed four catches for 111 yards and another TD, on a 26-yarder. Even though the Raiders lost the game, 34–28, they had found a receiver, Mike Siani . . . and lost one, Cliff Branch.

Lost to the bench, that is. Siani continued to play outstanding football for the rest of the year and Cliff remained his occasional caddy and a return man. The memory of the one dropped pass haunted him.

"You can't imagine how many hours of sleep I lost over that one play," Cliff said. "I've gone over every step, every detail and I still cringe when I come to the part where I miss the catch."

The fact that Cliff never got a chance to play regularly the rest of the year helped compound the nightmare. He was even somewhat of a disappointment on kick returns, hauling back nine for 191 yards and a 21.2 average. But his longest return was just 31 yards. And he lugged back 12 punts for just 21 yards and a 1.8 average. The pro game wasn't easy, and some people began wondering if

Cliff Branch wasn't just another one of those sprinters who couldn't make it.

The Raiders weren't disappointed, however. They regained the divisional title with a 10–3–1 mark and rookie receiver Siani contributed with 28 catches for 496 yards, five TD's, and a 17.7 average. He had an outstanding rookie year. Even though the team lost a heartbreaker to Pittsburgh in the playoffs, it was obvious they were among the best clubs in the league.

As for Cliff, he longed for a second chance. He needed his confidence back and one way to recapture some of it was a return to track. There was a young pro track circuit making the tour for the first time and it featured a new gimmick, a "King of the Hill" 40-yard dash for football players. And it featured Bob Hayes, the world's fastest human in the 1964 Olympics. Though approaching 30 years of age, Hayes was taking on all comers and whipping them—that is, until he met Cliff Branch.

Cliff flew up to Portland, Oregon, for the meet and promptly whipped Hayes by a yard, running a 4.4 40-yard dash. It was the first time in 14 meets that anyone had defeated the Cowboys' receiver.

"Sure, I felt good about that," Cliff said. "It was good competition, good to win. But if I can't win a job with the Raiders, what good is it."

Oh, yes, Cliff caught a few passes his rookie year. Three, to be exact. For 41 yards and no touchdowns. They weren't the kind of stats designed to put a player into the Hall of Fame. But he was young and resilient, and before the 1973 season was again talking about what he felt he should be doing for the team.

"The club didn't have a consistent deep threat as it had in the past with Warren Wells. I'm hoping to give the team what it had with Warren. I've watched a lot of films when Warren was here and I saw the things he did, the things the team did. I can feel the improvement already since I've come to camp. Funny, how a little experience helps. You start to feel you know a bit more about the whole thing. Now it's just a matter of getting some consistency and winning a job."

That wouldn't be easy. Biletnikoff was a fixture on one side, and Siani looked better than ever on the other. Sure enough, when the season began, Siani was still the starter and earning every penny of his pay.

It was another successful season for the Raiders, a 9–4–1 log and another divisional crown. It was also a big year for Biletnikoff and Siani, as the pair caught 48 and 45 passes respectively. But one thing was still missing . . . the long bomb. The two wide receivers had just seven touchdown catches between them.

As for Cliff it was another frustrating year. He saw just enough action to feel he merited a full shot, retaining and even building his confidence. Subbing for both wide catchers, Cliff grabbed 19 passes for 290 yards, a 15.3 average, and three touchdowns, as many as Siani had with more than twice as many catches.

This time the Raiders won their first playoff game against Pittsburgh, but were stopped by Miami for the AFC title. Once more the Super Bowl eluded the team, but they continued to add good players, their solid organization aiming toward 1974 without hesitation.

Cliff was back again, but this time with questions. Would he get more of a chance? Or, maybe, he was destined to remain a second stringer throughout his career? After all, the club didn't even have him returning kicks in '74. He still worked hard in training camp, but there were more lingering doubts than ever before.

Then in the pre-season Siani pulled a leg muscle, giving Cliff a chance for more playing time. Bang! Just like that he exploded. Three years of practicing patterns and catching the ball had done the job. He was sure of himself and his hands were much improved.

In the second-to-last pre-season game Cliff was really outstanding. Playing against the San Francisco 49ers he grabbed five passes for 112 yards, including one beautiful 74-yard TD pass from quarterback Ken Stabler, a pass in which Cliff beat a top cornerback, Bruce Taylor.

"I thought I'd bumped him too hard," said Taylor, "and I didn't want to be called for interference. So I let up a little. But you just can't hesitate on a guy with that much speed."

Cliff was overjoyed by the performance and his big TD catch. "Taylor didn't really touch me," he said. "I just sailed by him. The pass was perfect; I didn't even have to break stride."

By the end of the pre-season Cliff had 15 catches, the same number as Biletnikoff. Siani was just recovering from the muscle pull. Cliff was named the starter. This time he wasn't about to blow it.

He didn't. From game one it was obvious that Cliff had arrived. He played with ease and assurance, his steps purposeful, his ability total. There was no lack of confidence, no hesitancy. And quarterback Stabler sensed he had a reliable receiver from the start. He went to Cliff without question, whenever he felt the situation called for it.

After five weeks the Raiders were moving, heading for another title. And Cliff Branch, well, he had gone from the bottom to close to the top. He was tied for second among AFC catchers with 19, and his 329 yards led the conference. He already had three TD's, and he was going to get better. Raider receiving coach Tom Flores was ecstatic about his newest star.

"The big thing, of course, is that he's had the opportunity to show what he can do," said the coach. "He's learned to control his speed and study various defenses. All the speed in the world is not going to do any good unless you're able to adjust. Cliff has."

Nothing changed as the season progressed except that Cliff got better. Siani recovered from the muscle pull, but soon after sustained another injury and was placed on the disabled list. Cliff didn't have to worry about losing his job, but the way he was playing, there probably wasn't another receiver in the league who could take it from him.

After 12 games the Raiders were 10–2 and had clinched their seventh divisional title in eight years. Cliff was a big part of it. He had 56 receptions for 1,032 yards and 11 touchdowns, the best passcatching stats in the league.

"We've got the bomb back in Cliff Branch," said Coach Madden. "He really has been something. He's catching footballs all over the place for us and he keeps those defenses honest."

Cliff was a deep threat, all right. He had four receptions for more than 60 yards, but he caught the short ones, too. He was quickly becoming a complete receiver.

When it ended, the Raiders had the best record in pro football, a 12–2 slate, and Cliff checked in with 60 catches for 1,092 yards, an 18.2 average and 13 scores. His yardage and TD catches led the entire NFL. He was an all-pro selection in his first full season.

"I was worried too much last year," Cliff admitted. "I was thinking that as soon as I made a mistake I'd get the hook. There's no pressure on me now. I think I'm on my way to becoming a complete receiver."

There was little argument. In the playoffs Cliff was outstanding. He had three catches for 84 yards as the Raiders dethroned the Miami Dolphins, including one brilliant TD catch that put the game on ice.

Unfortunately, the old playoff jinx still had its hold on the team. Oakland lost to Pittsburgh in the AFC title game and was out of it once more.

Perhaps the Raiders lost the big one again, but they surely found a receiver, an explosive one, probably the fastest in the league. After waiting for so long to get a chance, Cliff Branch is not going to blow it. He'll work to stay on top, and chances are that he will.

Let's face it, no one is about to catch Cliff Branch.

Harold Jackson

There's an old saying in sports:

A good big man will beat a good little man most of the time.

Forget it! What about the likes of Phil Rizzuto, Ken Rosewall, Bob Cousy, and Gary Player? They're all players of smaller-than-average size from various sports who became stars and often had to match up with bigger men along the way.

It's the same story on the gridiron. Of course, in today's game, a 190-pounder couldn't play defensive tackle. No way. But a 245-pound tackle such as Alan Page can defeat players weighing up to 30 pounds more than he. So once the size ratio for a position is determined, the man at the bottom of the scale can certainly be as good as the man at the top.

Take the case of Harold Jackson, the explosive wide receiver of the Los Angeles Rams. Jackson is listed in the Rams' press guide at 5-10, and 175 pounds. Some say he's an inch or so smaller, and by the time the season is in full swing, some 10 pounds or so lighter.

He surely looks smaller than that on the field, for Harold Jackson likes to achieve the maximum speed and thus wears the minimum amount of protective padding. And when he goes into the team huddle, he'll likely be standing alongside 6-5 tight end Bob Klein or some other giant.

And when he runs his pass patterns, Harold is often dwarfed by linebackers and defensive backs inches taller and pounds heavier.

But then something happens. The pass is in the air, long and deep, and running under it, all alone, is Harold Jackson. And as he sprints into the end zone on another long touchdown play, Harold Jackson looks like the biggest man on the whole field.

Of course, Harold Jackson has never really worried about his size. It's always been the other guy who's worried about it. Take when Harold was drafted in 1968 by the Los Angeles Rams. He was just a twelfth-round choice and he spent the entire season sitting the bench.

The reason was simple. Then Ram coach George Allen liked big receivers and made no bones about it. So Harold didn't catch a single pass. A year later he was on his way to Philadelphia in one of the most one-sided trades in NFL history. Because in the course of one year, "little" Harold Jackson went from zero catches for zero yards to 65 catches for 1,116 yards and nine touchdowns. Instant all-pro.

Four years later he was on his way back to the Rams where new coach Chuck Knox had no qualms about a man's size. Jackson responded with another all-pro year in which he grabbed 13 touchdown passes from quarterback John Hadl. And that happened just at a time when people were saying the long bomb was dead, that zone defenses had taken it away. But more than anyone else, it was "little" Harold Jackson who took the zone defenses away from some teams.

Harold Jackson has never really had a bad season, nor has he lost any real time to injuries. He's durable as well as fast, disproving another theory about little guys, that they can't take it.

Harold is a quiet, unassuming man who really shuns the glamourous life, one he could quickly adopt playing in California. But in the off-season, he always returns to his native Hattiesburg, Mississippi, where his family still lives and his sisters and brother run a clothing store that Harold opened several years back. He becomes just another guy living a relaxing, peaceful, but productive life.

"I've always loved Hattiesburg," Harold says.

"It's a nice, clean little town of 70,000 or so with no problems and no grumbles. Nobody breaks in at night. You can relax and do what you want."

It's a tribute to the Jackson family that they've remained together and been so close a family unit. That can be a rare thing in today's world, and more often than not, the one who becomes the star rarely returns. But Harold has always been happy there and he's not about to forget it.

He was born on January 6, 1946, in Hattiesburg, of course. His parents were hard-working people who provided for and looked out for their large family. As expected, Harold had a happy childhood filled with fond and good memories. He recalls that even at an early age there was a big emphasis on running and speed.

"Running was kind of the thing to do in my neighborhood," he said. "If Mama asked you to go to the store for a loaf of bread you'd run to the store. Then we were always playing little games like who could run three or four blocks the fastest. It was really something big to be the fastest. I finally made the fastest about in the sixth grade."

Speed usually comes to the little guys, if for no other reason than as a device to run away from a big guy or two. Anyway, Harold was always small. That made it tough for him when he played sports with his friends, but he always hung in there and early on learned to use his speed to the best advantage.

When he entered Rowan High School in Hattiesburg, he weighed a little more than 120 pounds. That's skinny. But he still found his way right into the gridiron end zone . . . as a member of the school band!

Yep, that's how it was at first. Harold was a trumpet player in the school band. His parents had seen a football game and quickly concluded that the sport wasn't right for a 120-pound youngster. So it was the trumpet for the first two years.

But that didn't stop Harold from playing the sport in gym class.

"I'd come home with my knees ripped out of my pants and Mama would say, 'No more football!' The next day I'd come home with the knees ripped again. Finally she just threw up her hands in disgust."

It was the gym class touch games that first attracted attention to Harold. Until then, the school's football coaches knew nothing about him, just the skinny kid who played trumpet in the band. But when they watched him day after day running away from everyone and catching passes with ease, they began thinking. And pretty soon one of them even asked him to think about coming out for the team.

Finally, at the beginning of his senior year he did it. First, he had to put on 10 pounds to satisfy his parents, but as soon as he began playing with the varsity, it became obvious that it was no different from the gym classes. He still ran away from everybody and caught passes with ease. Before long the college scouts were starting to look him over.

One school that wanted him badly was Florida A & M, the school which Bob Hayes had played for. The coach there, Jake Gaither, saw Harold as the man to replace Hayes. There wasn't that much difference in their speed. Then another school entered the picture. It was Jackson State, located just 90 miles or so from Hattiesburg. That's what finally convinced Harold. He liked the idea of being fairly close to home and picked Jackson. It was Jackson to Jackson, as they say.

Becoming a star at Jackson State wasn't easy. The school played in a tough conference (Southwest Athletic Conference), one which produced an abundance of speed players at receiver, running back, and defensive back. Some of the defensive backs Harold had to go up against were Ken Ellis, Jim Kearney, and Willie Mitchell, all of whom made it big in the pros. He also had a couple of good ones on his team that he'd practice against, namely Lem Barney and John Outlaw.

And when Harold was starting the other wide receiver was Gloster Richardson, also a future pro, and brother of Willie Richardson, who preceded them at Jackson State and went on to all-pro status with the Baltimore Colts. So Jackson State wasn't a Mickey Mouse football school. Not at all.

At Jackson State, Harold managed to beef up

to around the 170-pound mark and still retained his 9.3 speed in the hundred. He also developed a style of his own. Even his number was different. He wore a double-zero (00) and had a song, "Double-0 Soul" which the band played whenever he made a great play, which was often.

Harold improved right into his junior year, and he cited the team's own practice sessions as the biggest factor in his improvement.

"Yeah, it all happened for me in practice, all right," he remembers. "Every play was a challenge. It would be me and Gloster running out for passes and Lem Barney and John Outlaw trying to stop us. Nobody wanted to be shown up by the other guy, even in practice. Yet we were all good friends and what happened is that we all made pretty good football players out of each other."

In his junior year Harold seemed well on his way to stardom. He was a gamebreaking receiver who could also run the short and medium patterns. He caught more than 50 passes that year and broke Willie Richardson's school receiving record. Despite his size, he was shaping up as a prime prospect for the pros.

Then in his senior year his luck ran out. He didn't return kicks very often, but on one occasion was sent back to field a punt. It was against archrival Alcorn A & M.

"The ball came to the other guy who was a few yards deeper than I was," Harold said. "But he fumbled it. I went back to pick it up and as I did they buried me from all sides. One guy grabbed my leg and tried to pull it off. Anyway, a ligament went and I was in a cast for six weeks."

Harold's activity was limited to just three games that year, severely diminishing his chances in the pro draft, and the amount of money he could command. The whole incident shows once again the great risks a professional athlete takes every time he steps on the field.

Anyway, Harold still awaited the draft. And as the rounds ticked away, nobody was calling his name. Finally, he was tabbed, on the 12th round by the Los Angeles Rams. It was better than nothing, and Harold reported to his first pro camp in July of 1968.

Harold was optimistic. He had a lot of reason to be. Despite the injury, he had prepared long and hard to get his chance.

"I can remember getting letters from pro teams when I was still a freshman at Jackson State," says Harold. "So I'd been thinking pro ball for a long time. I had some big games that people still talk about and I figured the pro teams must have heard about it.

"I also figured I was more than just a speed boy. A good flanker must be able to judge the ball, have a good set of hands, and the ability to maneuver, shifting the defensive back the way you want to. I've always played football and worked on my hands. I tried to catch all the balls I could and did a lot of finger exercises, like fingertip pushups, things like that.

"I know I'm small, but I'm not too small. I can compensate for lack of height. Heck, I once highjumped 6-3 in high school, so I can get up there. I want to play."

It was a good attitude to come into camp with, but unfortunately, George Allen was a coach with rigid attitudes. He had his own idea and did things his own way. One of those ways was to put big, strong receivers in the game. The coach looked at Harold in the pre-season, but played him in only four regular season games. And part of the time he didn't even dress since he was on the taxi squad. It was a long and frustrating year for him.

"Coach Allen was all for winning," Harold recalls. "Plus he liked the big guys. I remember getting in against the Bears, but it was mainly for decoy work. The last few minutes I flew down the field several times but got a little too far out of Gabe's (quarterback Roman Gabriel) reach. I always had to come back for the ball."

The result was absolutely no catches and a big question mark about the future. Not only did he see a dead end with the Rams, but he hadn't been able to show anything to the other teams. Who would want a guy who didn't catch a single pass and at first glance was no more than an undersized wide receiver? Harold began to think his pro career might be over before it had really begun.

That's when he got a break. The Rams had a veteran defensive back named Irv Cross, who was ending his playing career in L. A. that year. Cross worked against Harold in practice day after day and was one of the few men really impressed with the little guy.

"It was hard for me to believe that Harold wasn't playing," said Cross, "although that decision was up to Coach Allen. But when you get that kind of guy with good hands, moves and speed, you've got to take a long, serious look at him. I couldn't believe some of the moves he put on me. In fact, all the quarterbacks had trouble reaching him on the fly patterns. He got out there so quickly and moved so fast.

"When you get a flanker like Harold the first thing you do is look at his native ability . . . his speed, hands, maneuverability. Jackson was tops in all these areas."

But what could Irv Cross do? Nothing, at least not in 1968. But shortly after the season ended Cross retired as a player and was promptly hired as an assistant coach by his former team, the Philadelphia Eagles. Now he could do something. He immediately began bugging head coach Jerry Williams to go after Jackson in a trade.

In July, 1969, the deal was made. The Eagles sent fullback Izzy Lang to the Rams for Harold and a rookie defensive end named John Zook.

Zook was subsequently dealt to Atlanta, but the player transactions at this point get complicated. It was essentially a Lang-for-Jackson deal as far as Harold was concerned, and it soon turned into one of the most one-sided sports trades ever.

It quickly became evident that Harold would have a good shot at starting. "We fully anticipate Harold making a bid for the starting lineup," said Coach Williams. "He's a gamebreaking kind of player, just the kind of guy we need."

As for Harold, he was overjoyed by the trade.

"Yes, sir, I feel great about it," said Harold. "I don't know too much about the Eagles, but I just want a chance to make the squad."

Cross, the man who help bring Harold to Philly, couldn't say enough about him. "If you're looking for a guy who's tough, who won't be intimidated, who's willing to work and learn, then you've got your man. On the days we worked in shorts at L. A., Harold would be in full gear, running at top speed. He'd run and run and run some more. It seemed like he never wanted to leave the field."

Harold was a worker, all right, and it wasn't long before he was impressing everyone. In one of the first inter-team scrimmages at the end of July, Harold grabbed two 60-yard touchdown passes from Norm Snead, on both occasions simply outrunning the defensive back assigned to him. He caught a third pass that day and team observers were beginning to pencil him in as a starter. It was hard to see how he could be kept out of that line-up.

Sure enough, there was no way. When the 1969 season opened, Harold was at one wide receiving slot, while another good man, Ben Hawkins, manned the other spot. Veteran Gary Ballman was the tight end giving Philly three potential gamebreaking receivers on the field at the same time.

The Philadelphia team seemed forever in the throes of rebuilding. The club last won a championship in 1960, but there had been lean years ever since. There was a brief rebound to a 9–5 mark in 1966, but then things went bad again. In 1968 the club was last in its division with a 2–12 mark. There was really no place to go but up.

So Philly came out of the gate full of optimism. There were still problems, with the running attack, on defense, on the special teams. But the passing game was tops. Quarterback Snead was a veteran, and he didn't want to put too much pressure on any one of his catchers at the start. So he went to all of them equally. After three games, Hawkins had 13 catches, Ballman 11, and Harold was right there with 10, including one bomb, a 57-yard TDer.

"I always felt I could do the job," said Harold, "and I think things will get better. Even though I didn't get much game experience last year with the Rams, I did pick up a few good pointers. They always used me in practice to imitate the other team's best receiver. So one week I was Bob Hayes, the next week Clifton McNeil, then Paul Warfield, then Gene Washington. So I did the things all the speed guys were supposed to do, and since my game was speed, too, it helped me a lot."

As the season continued, Snead began looking more and more for the little guy . . . and finding him. Harold was becoming the team's most reliable receiver. He was also up near the top of the league in catches and total yardage. The Eagles still weren't winners, but with little Jackson in there, they were beginning to scare a whole lot of people.

The season ended with the Eagles a 4–9–1 team, up just a couple of notches from the year before. But Harold Jackson gave them respectability. He finished fourth in the entire NFL with 65 catches, while his 1,116 yards were tops in the league. He also scored nine TD's via the air route and had a 17.2 per catch average. It was an all-pro year, coming right after an all-nothing year. For Harold Jackson, that was quite an accomplishment.

He had showed it all, his speed, his moves, his catching ability, and his durability. Some people marveled at the fact that Harold wasn't hurt. After all, there are a lot of big guys who love nothing better than to cream little guys. But as one of the Eagles coaches said:

"Harold wasn't even hit hard once all year. He's so quick that the tacklers couldn't set him up for a full piece. And he's almost impossible to gang tackle because there's not a gang of tacklers quick enough to get to his area at the same time."

Before the 1970 season there was a problem with Harold's contract. He was earning close to the minimum when he joined the Eagles and wanted a substantial raise. General Manager Pete Retzlaff balked. He also balked with several other players, a dilemma that a team trying to rebuild couldn't afford. Harold still hadn't signed when the pre-season games began and found himself sitting the bench. That made him very angry.

"Sitting the bench is the only thing I hate about football," he said. "I like to be in there from the start so I can get warm and loose. I'm certainly not worried about my quality of play if I haven't signed. Once the game begins I don't think about money. And if we can't come to an agreement I'll still go out there and play the best football I can. They say they want me to improve my blocking. OK, I am working at it. But I'd really like to get this contract thing settled."

An agreement was finally reached, a compromise, and it still amounted to a nice raise from the year before. During the season the club tried to balance itself out. Much of the time they tried to establish a running game. Hence, there weren't as many passes filling the air lanes. Nor was there any improvement in the club. The scorecard was 3–10–1, and this time Harold caught 41 passes for

613 yards and five TD's. What that meant was another contract dispute before 1971.

It was getting to be a yearly thing. Harold's contention was two straight fine seasons plus talk that he'd be asked to run back some kicks this time. He remembered his punt return experience in college. For him, that scene required hazardous duty pay. But once again the problem was solved by compromise before the season started.

The Eagles had a new quarterback in Pete Liske during '71 and it took him awhile to establish a rapport with his receivers. Early in the season Liske concentrated on short stuff to his backs and to his big receivers, Ballman and Harold Carmichael. But when both of them were hurt, the QB was forced to look for Harold.

It was about midseason, but Harold hadn't lost anything. In two games he grabbed 16 passes, doubling his total of the first eight weeks. His yardage jumped from 184 to 386. The long play was back in the game.

"I enjoy running with the ball more than anything," said Harold. "What I really like is to catch one of those short passes, shake away from the first tackler and then go. Then you're running with the ball, cutting in and out, using blocks, faking guys. That's fun.

"I don't get that much of a thrill out of just running after a deep pass. I did a lot of that my first year in Philadelphia and it didn't excite me that much."

But it surely excited the fans. They buzzed everytime Harold burned off the line of scrimmage and the ball was thrown his way. After catching just 16 passes in the first eight games, Harold caught 31 in the final six to finish with 47 grabs for 716 yards. The club was 6–7–1 and seemed to be coming.

Unfortunately, the Eagles always have a way of turning things topsy-turvy. They came into 1972 looking to be in the divisional race. Then, bang. The team collapsed. The opener was an indication of things to come. The club lost to powerful Dallas, 28–6. The only bright spot was the play of Harold Jackson. He started his season by grabbing nine passes for 161 yards, a truly amazing performance in view of the beating the rest of the team took.

"I don't know what happened," said Harold. "We had a great practice and we were all psyched up. The whole scene reminded me of late last year when we were winning and things were going well. I thought it was a sign that we were gonna knock these guys off."

The rest of the season turned out to be just about the same. Harold Jackson against the world, and the Eagles on the losing side of the fence. Against Cleveland in the second game he had seven catches for 131 yards. He was burning everyone.

"I feel I'm more than just a speed merchant now," he said. "I can read the zones a lot better and I'm smarter. Pete (Liske) made me realize I should rely more on reading than on my speed, in other words, use my moves. In the beginning I'd try to outrun everybody and just run right into a crowd all the time."

Harold also learned to play hurt. His great game against Cleveland came with a badly-strained groin muscle which pained him severely. But that was part of the game.

"I've always been able to roll with the punches," Harold said. "The secret is not getting hit while your legs are planted. If you notice, my legs are always off the ground when I get hit. That way, the upper body doesn't go one way and the legs the other. I never give them a good piece of me. I just give them my moves."

The Eagles got off to a horrendous 1–6 start and the opposing teams got smart. The club had just one threat—Harold Jackson—so they concentrated on stopping him, and that meant double-teaming, triple-teaming, or whatever it took. It happened first against the Cardinals, and Harold was held to just one catch for 13 yards.

"They'd start with a linebacker right up on me, and the guy would go almost as deep as I did most plays. He stayed on me to shut off the short sideline pass. Then the cornerback would get me man to man. If I tried to go between them the safetyman would come over. That was three guys I had to beat out there. It seemed that everytime the ball was snapped the whole defense rotated toward me."

It didn't help that Hawkins and Ballman were injured and not going full speed. But Harold just hoped every team wouldn't play him that way. When Kansas City didn't, Harold promptly beat cornerback Jim Marsalis twice for two TD scores in a 21–20 upset. Marsalis is one of the roughest cornerbacks in the league. He continually used bump-and-run tactics, but Harold fought him off and got free.

"People have come up to me during the early part of the year and said they think I'll catch 110 or 120 passes this year," Harold said. "But that's not going to happen, not the way they're ganging up on me. I'll just go out there and hope for the best, and get what I can."

He did that all right. When it ended Harold led the NFL with 62 catches and 1,048 yards. The amazing thing was that he did it with a 2–11–1 team that scored just 145 points all year. Perhaps that explains the fact that Harold scored just four TD's during the campaign. But he had re-established himself as the most feared deep receiver in the game, a unanimous all-pro. His market value was at its peak.

And the value of the Eagles was at an all-time low. The owners and fans were disgusted. Once again there was an overhaul, with tough Mike McCormack taking over as coach. McCormack knew he had to start from scratch. He wanted a strong quarterback, preferably a veteran, who could take charge of the offense and make it work. In June of 1973 the opportunity came. The Rams were willing to deal Roman Gabriel to the Eagles. He was the man McCormack wanted. But the price would be high. To get Gabe, the Eagles would have to trade Harold Jackson.

After thinking it over, the Eagles said yes. So Harold was on his way back to the team that drafted him, going over along with running back Tony Baker and a couple of draft picks, all for Gabriel. The deal would work out well for both teams.

As for Harold, he enjoyed his stay in Philly, but was also happy to be with a winner.

"I think I was the only guy the fans in Philly never booed," he said. "But I'm very happy to be back with the Rams. They're winners and they've got a great veteran quarterback in John Hadl. It did become frustrating in Philly after awhile. You just can't help but get tired of losing."

The Rams were a different team than when Harold was there the first time, though just five years had passed. There was a new coach in Chuck Knox and many new faces. And this time there was no talk about Harold's size. His great record at Philly did the talking for him, and reporters flocked around the little receiver during the pre-season to ask him a basket of questions about passcatching.

"In a way, little guys have the edge in pass offense today," Harold said. "People talk about big targets, but what the passer wants is an open target, and I've learned to get open.

"Sure, zone defenses have hurt some guys. But I got zoned on almost every play last year and still led the league. All you have to do is get between the defensive backs, and if you don't carry around too much height and weight, you can do that, if you're quick enough.

"Plus the quarterback never has any trouble finding me. Look at it this way. A 6-3 receiver in a crowd of 6-3 linebackers is harder to see than a 5-10 receiver who is off by himself somewhere."

Then someone asked about another defensive maneuver that came in about the same time as the zone, that being the bump-and-run tactics used by many defenders.

"I like it when they try the bump and run stuff," said Harold. "I feel I can outrun any man on my head to begin with, and if he tried to bump me, then I've really got him. The reason for that is that I can usually avoid the hit with my speed, and in trying to hit me, the defender is throwing himself off balance. When he recovers, I'm gone."

Then Harold went out and put his theories into practice. The Rams were a much-improved team in '73, one of the best in the league. And it didn't take long for Harold to begin perking with veteran John Hadl. Hadl liked to throw long anyway, having tossed passes to the great Lance Alworth during his years at San Diego. And in Jackson, he had a receiver who could do it all.

The two really came into their own as a combo in mid-October, when the Rams met the always-tough Dallas Cowboys. The Cowboys were good, all right, but on that particular Sunday they just couldn't stop the Hadl to Jackson combination. Little Harold gathered in seven passes for a whopping 238 yards as he drove the Dallas defenders to distraction with his dazzle. Four of the tosses went for touchdowns, and they came from distances of 67, 63, 36, and 16 yards.

Harold admitted it was his best performance as a pro, and QB Hadl just couldn't say enough about him.

"Harold is definitely the best deep receiving threat in the league," said John. "He has fantastic hands, fantastic speed, and a fantastic ability to get open."

That's how it was most of the year. Whenever the Rams were in a tough spot, Hadl went to Jackson. Yet the club also had a fine running attack and didn't have to throw all the time. So there wasn't the same kind of defensive pressure on Harold as there had been that last year in Philly.

When it all ended the Rams had regained the divisional title with a 12–2 mark, and Harold had completed another all-pro year with 40 catches for 874 yards, a fantastic 21.9 average, and a league leading 13 touchdowns. He was simply amazing.

Unfortunately, the team faded in the playoffs, losing to Dallas, 27–16, but Harold was finally with a big winner and it felt good.

The club had a few problems in '74, namely at quarterback, where a mid-season trade sent John Hadl to Green Bay and handed the job to young Jim Harris, who, because of his inexperience played a rather conservative game. They retained their divisional title with a 10–4 mark, but Harold didn't have the same kind of stats, catching just 30 passes for 514 yards and five TD's.

"We did a little more running than we normally do," said Harold, "but we established a pretty solid running game so it was worth it. So on many occasions we ran certain pass patterns where I clear out. Not exactly as a decoy, just taking guys out of there."

This time the team had a bit better luck in the playoffs. They whipped Washington, 19–10, in the first round, but then lost to Minnesota, 14–10, in the NFC title game. It was another disappointment, but the club was getting closer and the optimism remains.

Another thing that remains is Harold Jackson, still regarded as one of the most dangerous deep threats in the game. With Harold in there, any given play can result in a touchdown. That makes Coach Knox very happy. And he's glad to have Harold Jackson on his team.

"Would you believe that Harold is our disaster quarterback," Knox said one day. "That means if both our regular signalcallers were injured in the same game, Harold would take over. Surprise you? It shouldn't. Harold is about the best all-around athlete on the squad. I'd trust him in any emergency situation. He's also a joy to be around. His attitude towards his job, towards his teammates, and everybody else is perfect."

Notice one thing. Chuck Knox didn't say a word about Harold Jackson being too small.

Riley Odoms

Riley Odoms. His name *sounds* like the name of a tight end. That he is, one of the bright new stars at the position in the NFL. Riley Odoms stands 6-4 and plays at about 238 pounds. That's big and strong, and that's what tight ends must be in today's game.

They must also be fast, since in recent years they have become increasingly important as primary receivers throughout the league. Odoms plays for the Denver Broncos. After just three seasons with the Broncs he was being named on several all-pro teams.

There was a time when picking the all-pro tight end was easy. That's because there were just a few outstanding ones around. Now there are many. Besides Odoms, perennial candidates for all-pro tight end include Bob Tucker, Ted Kwalick, Charles Young, Charlie Sanders, Raymond Chester, Rich Caster, Bob Trumpy, Jim Mandich, Jerry Smith, and Jim Mitchell.

Thanks to zone defenses and tighter coverage of wide receivers, tight ends have come into their own as passcatchers. For instance, in 1974, the two longest pass plays in the AFC and NFC were made to tight ends; an 89-yarder to the Jets' Rich Caster and an 81-yarder to the Cards' Jackie Smith. It's more than coincidence.

And there are other facts. Several years ago, Bob Tucker of the Giants became the first tight end ever to win a conference receiving title over an entire season. In 1974, it happened again, this time Charles Young of Philadelphia leading the NFC with 63 receptions.

Riley Odoms fits right in with these new-breed, passcatching tight ends. In both 1973 and 1974, the big Bronco snared 43 passes, good for 629 and 639 yards respectively. In those seasons he scored seven, then six touchdowns, a remarkable record of consistency.

But like the other top tight ends, Riley Odoms is more than just a wide receiver moved in tight to the line. He has to be, for the traditional role of the tight ends hasn't changed, it's just expanded.

Here's how one writer described the position in

a magazine article which also talked about the expanded role of the tight end.

"The ideal tight end is big enough to block a 270-pound defensive end, agile enough to block a 230-pound linebacker, and quick enough to block a 190-pound defensive halfback. He is sturdy enough to catch a pass over the middle, in the heart of combat, and swift enough to sprint downfield on a fly pattern. He must have great hands, immense courage, uncommon running ability—and enough intelligence to keep straight his wide variety of roles."

Some of the tight ends excel at one particular phase of the game. Caster, for example, has the speed to run with any defensive back in the league and his quarterback, Joe Namath, loves to throw to him deep. Miami's Mandich is a great clutch receiver who Bob Griese goes to in key third-down situations. Veteran Milt Morin of Cleveland has always been utilized for his blocking ability. Bob Tucker, though he can do all the other things, is a crack runner once he has the ball.

Some of the others, like Sanders, Kwalick, and Chester, can do everything well. Riley Odoms fits into this category. He's younger than the others, and still improving. Many think he is just a year or two away from being the best tight end in the league.

None of these men, however, might be getting the action and notoriety if it hadn't been for two former greats of the gridiron. They are Ron

Kramer, a tight end known as "The Big Oaf," and his coach, the late Vince Lombardi of the Green Bay Packers.

Kramer came into the league in the later 1950's after an all-America career at the University of Michigan. He was a 6-3, 250-pound giant, but when he came to the pros he rapidly slipped into the realm of the mediocre. He was a tight end, but he really wasn't doing much to help his team and there was talk of his being cut.

Then Lombardi took over as coach in 1959. He looked at his rag-tag collection of last-place losers, picked up a nearby football, and said:

"This, gentlemen, is a football. Before we're through, we're gonna ram it down everybody's throat!"

There was a lot of long passing in the NFL game of the '50's, most of it featuring speedy wide receivers. Lombardi wanted to use more of a running game. He took one look at Kramer's size, remembered he was also an all-America basketball player with great mobility, and decided that he'd be perfect for the kind of game the coach wanted.

The early tight ends didn't always play in close to the line, so many of them barely weighed more than 200 pounds. They couldn't handle a blocking assignment without help from the tackle alongside them. But Lombardi wanted to run sweeps, and that meant his tight end had to be able to take a man out by himself, whether he be tackle, linebacker, or defensive back.

So Kramer gave Lombardi an extra blocker and in two years became an all-pro at his position. And blocking wasn't all he did. Lombardi quickly found a way to get maximum mileage from Kramer. On certain key third-down situations he'd have Kramer fake a block, then slip over the middle. Soon quarterback Bart Starr found he had another reliable receiver to throw to. Kramer averaged 35 catches a year during his tenure with the Packers, who went on to become world champions and one of the greatest teams ever. And amidst all that, the modern tight end was born.

They began coming into the league quickly then, built along the lines of Kramer, and other NFL coaches began using the Lombardi system. Soon tight ends like Monte Stickles, Mike Ditka, and John Mackey began bringing new respect and new skills to the position. And after them, came the men who are playing today.

Sometimes it seems as if tight ends have more trouble coming into their own than players at other positions, further testimony to the complexity and multiple skills they must acquire. College training isn't always enough. Bob Tucker kicked around semi-pro ball for two years and was cut from two pro teams before making it. Kwalick was everybody's all-America at Penn State then caught just 12 passes in two years at San Francisco before making it big. Even Mackey, voted the best tight end in the NFL's first 50 years, was almost switched to fullback before being turned loose at tight end for keeps.

It didn't come easy for Riley Odoms, either. He spent his first two years at the University of Houston playing second string to a man named Earl Thomas, who, incidently, is still struggling to become a starter with the St. Louis Cardinals. And unlike most superstars, Riley seemed content to remain number two, never quite having the confidence in himself and figuring there was no way to beat Thomas out.

Once in the pros Riley had another battle to fight. As a rookie he was plagued by some self-doubts, and fortunately, Coach John Ralston recognized it and brought him along slowly, alternating him with veteran Billy Masters his rookie year. This allowed Riley time to adjust with minimal pressure, and in his second year he finally emerged, establishing his position alongside the others as one of the top tight ends in the league. And since he is playing with an up-and-coming team, the future surely seems bright.

Riley Odoms was born in Luling, Texas, on March 1, 1950, and he grew up in nearby Corpus Christi. He was a happy-go-lucky youngster who freelanced through his early years, doing pretty much what he wanted. He played a lot of sports with his friends, but never really took sports seriously. Riley just sort of drifted with the winds, having fun and exhibiting tremendous loyalty to his friends.

He was a big kid by then, but never really threw his weight around. By the time he reached high school he excelled at all the sports, but didn't really have the killer instinct, win-at-all-costs kind of attitude that many future stars acquire early.

"I used to do just about anything that popped into my mind," Riley recalls. "No one could predict what I'd do next, not even me. For example, I might see some girl I didn't even know and yell, 'Hey, Fatty!' I guess I was just too frank. I was quiet most of the time, but sometimes I might get a sudden notion to do or say something and just go ahead."

Riley wasn't a mean person. His sudden impulsive notions weren't intended to do harm. He himself admits he just didn't think before he acted sometimes, a trait that had to do with growing up. But all Riley's impulses weren't like the one above.

When he reached West Oso High School he became an all-state star in football and basketball, and was also state high jump champ. As for baseball, well, that's where Riley's impulsive actions entered again. He was en route to an all-state season in baseball, playing first base and hitting the ball a country mile when he connected.

He had a good friend, Billy Ray Nelson, who happened to be the second-string first baseman behind Riley. There were some times when Riley had to go to track meets and Nelson would get a chance to play. But when Riley came back, Nelson was returned to the bench. This bothered Riley.

He didn't like seeing his friend shuttled around like that. So one day he just up and quit.

"I liked baseball and played pretty well. But I figured I was doing real well in track and at the same time was fouling up Billy's season. So I figured I'd quit baseball so he could play every day. I just wanted to be fair to him."

So that was still another side of Riley Odoms. He didn't give his position to anyone on the football team and he kept his grades up. So when he graduated he accepted a scholarship to the University of Houston, not a major football school, but a good one.

Upon entering Houston, Riley found his attitude hadn't really changed. He was still impulsive and some of the things he did hurt him.

"There was one time when we missed a bed-check in mid-season and three of us were suspended for a couple of games. The same old story, I just didn't think before I did it. In a lot of ways those were discouraging days, but they just made me a little older, and that was good."

Riley had a good freshman year. He was at his full height and beefing up all the time. But when he arrived for varsity practice as a sophomore he found junior Earl Thomas ahead of him. It was the beginning of two frustrating years for him.

"At first I didn't care if Earl was number one," recalls Riley, "I just went out to play my sophomore year. But I just went down. I don't really know what it was. I guess I saw I never could beat him out. We were good friends, but I knew Earl was the starting tight end and I knew nothing I could do would change that."

It was a bad situation, one that undoubtedly retarded Riley's development. He quickly got the reputation of a player not playing up to his potential. It was a tough thing for Coach Bill Yeoman to watch.

"Maybe I should have redshirted Riley for one year," said the coach. "That would have given him an extra year after Earl left. But I didn't do it. You don't always know how a kid will accept a redshirt. All kids don't have instant maturity, and I decided to keep Riley on the varsity."

So Riley began two years of being Earl Thomas' occasional caddy. He didn't play much at all his sophomore year and saw no more action as a junior. In fact, during the 1970 season he played only 42 minutes all year, catching just five passes for 50 yards and a single touchdown.

It was a discouraging time for Riley. Fortunately he didn't fall apart completely. A lesser man could have found himself back on the streets. But Riley kept his grades up and looked to the future, whether football was in it or not.

"I planned to get my degree, even if it took an extra semester or so," he said. "I wasn't sure exactly what I was going to do, but I knew I enjoyed working with young kids. I found that out by working summers in the city recreation department in Corpus Christi.

"You can be an engineer or doctor and make all kinds of money for yourself. But most young black kids dream of being somebody like Gale Sayers or Jim Brown. So I can help them find out just who they are and what they can be, if they have the potential to try it in football. The game has changed so much that they need all the help they can get."

Riley returned to Houston for his senior year and for the first time there was no Earl Thomas ahead of him. The coaches still looked upon him as a player with great potential. Coach Yeoman wanted to give him confidence and told him the job was his as long as he could keep it.

During the pre-season Riley worked well and kept his hold on the job. Then, in two early season games he suddenly emerged with 15 catches and three touchdowns. His confidence finally had the shot in the arm it needed. Coach Yeoman remembers it well.

"When you get in that end zone you walk a little different," said the coach. "I could see the change right after those two games. Riley had finally proved to himself that he could do the job. He was on his way."

By midseason Riley was getting press for the first time, and the pro scouts began coming out to see just where this human bulldozer had been hiding for two years. Not only could Riley catch the ball, but he was a vicious blocker on running plays and figured prominently in the Houston offense.

The club was very good in 1971. Before the year ended they'd lost just two games, to powerhouses Alabama and Arizona State. And in those games Riley Odoms continued to stand out, catching three of his eight touchdown passes against those top teams.

The Houston offense was a balance of running and passing. The club had a fine fullback in Bobby Newhouse and let him handle the bulk of the running game. Riley never carried on an end around. But in passing situations the backs never ran a pass route. They stayed back to block, because Riley Odoms was target enough. He was the man they went to in almost every clutch situation.

In fact, when the club wanted to go long, they often split Riley out wide, using his great speed, enabling him to pick up some long gainers including one beautiful 68-yard pass-run touchdown play.

Riley had to be a fast learner. After all, he saw little action his first two years and missed that valuable playing time that gives experience and gridiron saavy. In many ways he was raw and rough in his pattern work. But his natural ability carried him to a season of 45 receptions for 730 yards and eight TD's. He was an all-America selection on most ballots and talked about as the best pro prospect at his position in the country.

This opinion was fortified after he performed well at the Astro-Bluebonnet Bowl. Some scouts were calling him another John Mackey, noting the strong physical resemblance between the two. And his own coach, Bill Yeoman, after two years of frustration with Riley, said this:

"Riley is quicker than most wide receivers and stronger than most tackles. He has the kind of body tight ends of the future will want to measure up with. Besides that, he can catch the football."

Yeoman's respect for Riley came hard, but once it was there, the coach was a diehard Riley Odoms fan. In fact, shortly after the 1971 season ended, a sportswriter asked several college coaches about a "reverse draft," in other words, gave them the pick of any one pro football player, rookie or veteran, to have on their college teams. Most of the coaches named the likes of Dick Butkus, Lee Roy Jordan, Sonny Jurgensen, Paul Warfield, and O. J. Simpson. Not Bill Yeoman.

"You couldn't ask me an easier question," said the coach. "I wouldn't even consider a lot of the stars. I'd just take Riley Odoms. Just give me Odoms back and I'd be the happiest coach in the country."

So there was no doubt on what terms player and coach parted company. Now Riley awaited the pro draft. It was obvious that he'd be a high pick. In fact, the New York Jets had already made it public that they were looking for a tight end and that Riley Odoms was the man they wanted. So for once, it looked as if Riley were in the driver's seat. Things were going his way.

Those who figured Riley would go high were

right. He was the fifth collegian picked, and the number one choice of the Denver Broncos of the American Conference. Some said it wasn't a banner year for draft choices (the number one pick of the entire league was a lineman named Walt Patulski), but Riley had to be proud. He had had, in effect, just one full year of college ball, and now he was the fifth collegian in the entire country picked by the pros.

For that reason, Riley wasn't about to enter into a long contract hassle, especially after the Broncos initial offer turned out to be a substantial one. Though represented by an agent, Riley and the Broncs came to terms in just four hours, an uncommonly short negotiation time for a number one choice. In fact, Riley was the first number one choice among all the teams to put his signature on a pro contract. The pact was for four years, estimated to be in the $200,000 range, with bonus and incentive clauses thrown in.

After the signing there were kind words on each side. Riley had never been happier.

"I can't wait for the season to open," he exclaimed. "Everything here is just beautiful, beautiful. I love the city, the stadium, and the climate. I want to live here and I love being on a team that's building. I know the feeling from Houston. We got better right into my senior year. It makes you really proud because you've been a part of it from the beginning and have seen it succeed.

"My objective here will be to earn respect as a

player. To do that, you've got to perform on the field. So my first aim is to make rookie of the year and I feel I can do it if I apply myself."

Bronco assistant coach Stan Jones said everyone connected with the team was happy about getting Odoms. "He's the best tight end I've seen in at least a couple of years. I know he's going to help us win some ballgames."

Later, when Riley faced reporters for the first time, he talked about his career and about his type of game.

"Last year at Houston meant everything to me," he said. "I was lucky because I got a chance to play regularly and I had a great coaching staff to help me. Our receiver coach, Joe Arenas, taught us so much, how to run patterns and how to protect the ball with your body when you're going to be hit.

"I also worked hard at my blocking in college. If you can't block, you can't play tight end, and I always try to keep my blocking on the same level as my catching. As for catching, my favorite pattern at Houston was over the middle with the hopes of man-to-man coverage. You can't argue when you've got just one man to beat to get open."

Of course, Riley wasn't going to be handed the starting job at Denver. The holdover tight end was Billy Masters, who had done a good job for the club in 1971. So Riley would have to beat Masters out if he wanted to start. But he'd lose some training camp time. In July, he traveled to Chicago to play in the College All-Star Game.

As usual, the pros won, the champion Dallas Cowboys whipping the college stars, 20–7. And, as usual, the game proved a good education for those collegians who saw sustained action. The collegians had quarterback problems as neither Jerry Tagge nor Pat Sullivan could move the team. As a result, Riley didn't catch a single pass, but he was satisfied.

"The important thing is that I felt I could compete with them," he said. "They're the best in the NFL but they didn't really surprise us with anything. I thought they'd try some tricks on me, holding stuff, but they didn't. They played a very clean game.

"Our passing attack never really got started. I was the primary receiver on only three or four deep patterns and one curl. The one time I was really open the ball came over my wrong shoulder, and that was a matter of not coordinating with the quarterback.

"I'm not worried about catching up when I get back to Denver," he said. "The delay will bother me only in knowing the plays and in timing with the quarterbacks. I'm in good shape and around my playing weight of about 235."

So Riley rejoined his new teammates in Denver. He was joining a club that had been an American Football League original back in 1960, and had experienced many long, frustrating years since then. In fact, the Denver Broncos had never had a winning season throughout their history. The best was a 7–7 log in 1962. But the year before that they were 3–11, and the year after 2–11–1. So even that single .500 season seemed to be a fluke.

The team had a few outstanding players, but could never seem to field a solid offensive and defensive team at the same time. And there was never much depth. The fans in the Mile High City were longing for a winner.

In an attempt to shake things up, the Denver people brought in a new head coach for the 1972 season. He was John Ralston, fresh from the college ranks where he coached at Stanford, and a man with his own ideas about running a football team.

Ralston is an optimist, a positive thinker, a man who always looks at the bright side of things.

"What you've got to understand," he said, shortly after arriving in Denver, "is that I actually *see* myself coaching in the Super Bowl. I've *got* to see it. It's just like it was with the Rose Bowl. Talk about an obsession with something. I had this total, all-encompassing obsession to get to the Rose Bowl."

Well, Ralston got there, not once, but twice. And if that was any indication, the fans of Denver had something to look forward to. And Ralston wasn't kidding about his attitude. Even before his first Denver team took the field in 1972, Ralston said, "We're going to win ten, lose four, and play in the Super Bowl."

A joke? To some, maybe. But that's the way John Ralston believed. And he immediately set out to give his players the same feeling. Of course, it takes awhile to make believers out of skeptical veterans. So while Ralston may have had his heart set on a winning season, many longtime Bronco watchers figured he'd be lucky to break even.

It was worse than that. After an opening victory over the Houston Oilers, the mistakes began coming, and they came in the form of four straight losses. But an upset of mighty Oakland broke the spell. The other victories came against Los Angeles, San Diego, and New England. But that was all. The team checked in with a 5–9 record and the skeptics said I-told-you-so.

The year also had to be something of a disappointment for Riley. Though he worked hard right from the start, the coaches felt it best to start Masters and alternate with Odoms. In fact, for part of the year, Coach Ralston used his tight ends as "messengers," shuttling them on every play and having both of them bring in the next play from the bench. That can be a frustrating method for both players, but neither complained and each produced good football.

When the season ended, Masters had 25 receptions for 393 yards and three scores, while Riley checked in with 21 catches for 320 yards and one score. That meant the Denver tight ends grabbed 46 passes for more than 700 yards.

"It was hard to choose between the two men," said one writer who had followed the team. "They are about the same size and both catch the ball well. But Odoms seems to be the better blocker and he's a lot faster. Besides, Masters is 28, Odoms just 22. And Riley can only get better. The Bronco future seems to be with him."

There were some important things happening despite the 5–9 record. The team found itself a reliable quarterback in veteran Charley Johnson, many of the younger players such as Riley got valuable experience, and John Ralston won the confidence of his players.

"Coach Ralston is our number one cheerleader," said longtime running star Floyd Little. "I'll never forget a long run I made against the Giants in Yankee Stadium. Here I am, coming around the right end. I break down the sidelines and all of a sudden there's John, running right along with me. He runs all the way to the goal line with me, with his clipboard and everything. And after I score, he's the first one to throw his arms around me."

So by methods some considered corny, the coach was instilling a new kind of team spirit among the Broncos. And when 1973 began, Ralston again predicted a winning year and onto the Super Bowl. He also had some important coaching decisions to make, not the least of which was what to do about his tight end situation. For in the pre-season games Riley Odoms was looking very good.

Ralston had said he wanted a number one tight end for '73, so there was a great deal at stake. The situation simplified itself when Masters came down with a viral infection during training camp. When he finally got into a pre-season game he suffered a back injury. That made Riley Odoms the starting tight end.

The 1973 season began just like the year before. The club whipped Cincinnati in the opener, then lost three straight. In game five the club was losing to Houston, 20–10. A loss here and you could kiss the season goodbye. But somehow the team rallied and went on to win, 48–20. Coach Ralston says that game signalled the change in Bronco fortunes.

The next week the club rallied again, this time to tie Oakland. After that came wins over Pittsburgh and Kansas City and a six-week stretch in which the team was unbeaten, winning four and tying two. The streak put the team back into playoff contention, and it also showed fans everywhere that Riley Odoms was on the brink of becoming a star.

During that six-week period quarterback Johnson began going to Riley in more and more clutch situations. And the big guy responded with 23 receptions during that period, including four touchdowns. It made him the leading receiver among AFC tight ends with 28 for the year to date.

"I think Riley's fine play has been typical of

the growth and development of the Broncos this year," said Coach Ralston. "At this point, I wouldn't trade him for any other tight end in the league. When we drafted him we felt he was all-pro material, and I think he's getting pretty close to that right now."

There was tremendous excitement in Denver as the final week of the season approached. The Broncos were 7–4–2 and would be playing the Raiders. If they could beat Oakland, Denver would win the AFC Western title. But the club got a bad break early. Quarterback Johnson was injured, and with him out of there, the offense sputtered. Oakland took a 14–10 lead, and when Ralston gambled with a fake punt, the Raiders took advantage and scored the clinching TD to win it, 21–10.

Yet the team had finally cracked the .500 mark, finishing at 7–5–2, with high hopes for things to come.

Riley Odoms also had high hopes, for he had showed he could cut the mustard with the best of them with 43 catches for 629 yards and seven scores. But there were other young tight ends making a mark, notably rookie Charles Young of Philadelphia, who had caught 55 passes his first year and was named Rookie of the Year, in addition to making many all-pro teams. When a reporter mentioned this to Riley, stating that Young's success had helped mask Riley's fine season, young Mr. Odoms replied with level-headedness and his new-found maturity.

"My only goal during the past season was making the Pro Bowl game, and I did that. I never thought much about making any all-AFC teams or any all-pro teams, but I'm glad I made a few. No, I'm not jealous of Charley Young. His team throws more often, so there is more opportunity for him to make catches.

"He might be a little faster than I am, but I think I'm stronger. I'm built on a much heavier scale than he is. He sometimes gives the impression of being a quick, thin man. I give the impression of being a plodder, but I'm not.

"I think a lot of defensive backs look at me and see more of a tackle than an end, and I can get by them because my speed is much better than they think. That's my edge."

Then someone asked the inevitable question. What about the old rap about Riley not playing up to his potential, about lacking self-motivation.

"I never considered that a problem," he answered quickly. "A lot of other people did, though. In college, I did a few stupid things off the field and it resulted in a suspension once. But here no one worries about what we do off the field. Coach Ralston is a beautiful man. He even makes practice fun. But I like to feel that I've learned from all the things that I've done in college and in the pros.

"For one thing, I've learned that you have to

keep proving to others and to yourself that you are better than the next guy. When you stop trying to do that, you won't be better, no matter what kind of physical ability you might have."

So that's how Riley played it in '74. The Broncos were expected to be strong contenders for the title. They added a new regular halfback, Otis Armstrong, who became the NFL's rushing champion, and Riley was as good as ever with another 43 catches. But there was a players' strike before the season and the club got off to a bad start.

"All the clubs were in the same boat after the strike," said Riley, "but I think we burned ourselves out a little too much trying to make up for lost time. By the time we got going it was too late."

That was in the second half of the season and by then the Raiders had wrapped up the divisional crown. The Broncos came on strong for another winning season, but just barely at 7–6–1.

Yet there is still a bright future in Denver. The fans were always loyal, even during the lean years. Now, they're rabid with enthusiasm. There is a nucleus of fine players and a coach who thinks win, win, win. And there is also a tight end in Denver who has made it big. His name is Riley Odoms.

There had to be times when Odoms-watchers didn't think it would happen, but the big kid never really doubted himself, not after his senior year in college. Once he got the chance he proved it to himself and to everyone else. Now he's determined to prove it again and again.

For Riley Odoms is part of a tradition, the tradition of the tight end. He's also one of the new breed, in the forefront of a group of very talented athletes who have made this very complex and difficult position one of the glamour spots on the gridiron. For the tight end has to do it all—run, block, catch, decoy. And Riley Odoms does it as well as anyone in the NFL.

Charley Taylor

In 1974, Charley Taylor, the great wide receiver of the Washington Redskins caught 54 passes for 738 yards. The year before, in 1973, the same Taylor grabbed 59 for 801 yards. Pretty good statistics by any standards.

Very good statistics when you consider that Charley Taylor will be 34 years old when the 1975 season gets under way. Most pass receivers are out of the game by that stage of their lives, or, if they're still playing, have been reduced to part-timers or at best, shadows of their former selves.

Not Charley Taylor. He's still going strong, still slick and smooth, still one of the most feared receivers in the entire league. In fact, through 1974,

Charley has corralled some 582 passes in his career, good for third place on the all-time list, and since the leader, Don Maynard, has 633, another strong year or two could make Charley the NFL's all-time standard bearer in the receiving department.

In a way, it's a minor miracle that Charley Taylor is still playing first-rate football. He had his rib cage rearranged while still in high school, then suffered a potentially fatal broken neck his first varsity season at Arizona State. He recovered to play again, but once in the pros sustained a broken ankle his second year, a broken hand a few years later, plus more than his share of pulled muscles, sprains, and assorted bumps and bruises.

When he played in the College All-Star game before his rookie year he was called lazy by his coach. He began his pro career as a running back and two years later was switched to wide receiver. Don't position changes usually mean a player isn't really making it? He's also survived losing years in Washington and a succession of coaching changes.

Yet somehow, Charley Taylor has survived and prospered, gaining stature and respect all along the way. He's not as dynamic or explosive as some of the other top receivers in the league; he's not as fast or as big as some others. But Charley Taylor knows how to get free and catch the ball. He does it well and he does it consistently. In other words, Charley Taylor is a winner.

Charley's manner is often loose and casual, a factor that used to contribute to the idea that he didn't really take the game seriously. But although he didn't look like the worrying kind, he was. In fact, when he was switched from running back to wide receiver he worried incessantly about his future in football, and went on to become one of the most dedicated athletes in the game. You have to be dedicated to have completed 11 years in the violent world of the NFL.

There was no real way to predict superstardom for Charley Taylor early in his life. In fact, his accomplishments right through his college years were on a par with so many other players across the land, players who became NFL mediocrities or didn't make it at all.

The Charley Taylor story started in Grand Prairie, Texas, where he was born on September 28, 1941. Grand Prairie is very close to Dallas, so Charley was always quite near big-time football tradition. As he grew up he followed the many college teams in the area, but also spent time playing baseball and basketball.

When Charley entered Dalworth High School, an all-black institution in Grand Prairie, the school had just been elevated from grade-school only to include the secondary grades. Therefore the entire football program was completely new and wasn't the best organized around.

Charley was a big kid then, already standing six feet tall and weighing about 175 pounds as a freshman. His first position was tackle, but it wasn't because he was the biggest guy.

"We had a lot of big guys," he said. "In fact, I was about the lightest guy. It was just that everyone spoke his mind about the position he played and by the time they got to me, all the other spots were filled. I became a tackle by default."

It wasn't long afterward that Charley suffered his first serious injury. He landed hard on his side with several other players on top of him. His entire rib cage was badly damaged and the injury left him with a wheezing cough that lasted several years. Even today there is evidence of that injury. The right side of his chest and stomach area doesn't protrude as much as his left side.

The injury really shook up his parents. Charley was raised by his mother and stepfather, James Stevenson. Both wanted him to give up football after his injury and concentrate on baseball and track. It took a lot of persuading on Charley's part to convince his parents that the gridiron was his first and only real love. Finally, they agreed to let him return.

So Charley was back for his sophomore year. This time there was more organization and tryouts for each position. Charley did some thinking.

"I said to myself, an end job looks good. I'm not a glory hound but there's absolutely no praise for an inside lineman. We didn't have much running, but we passed a lot. So I said, 'Charles Taylor, you're an end.' "

That lasted one year. The next time around, his junior year, Charley was a fullback. That gave him a chance to imitate his idol, the great Cleveland fullback, Jim Brown. But there were other things troubling Charley then. He figured his football career was about over again, this time for another reason. He didn't feel he wanted to go to college. He wasn't sure what he would do, but he had nine, yes, nine uncles in the Air Force and thought he might like to follow in their footsteps.

Fortunately, Charley's stepfather was a thoughtful man who wanted the best for his stepson. Mr. Stevenson married Charley's mother when Charley was eight, but he loved the boy as if he was his own.

"I was a little shy of him at first," Charley remembers, "but he would always sit down and talk to me. You did some fool thing and he would warn you about it. He never hit out at you right away like some flesh-and-blood fathers do. He had a calm way of letting you know the next time you tried to jump the neighbor's hedges would be once too often. Anyway, he thought college was a good idea for me, the best idea, and he talked about it often. So I played football again as a senior, worked hard, and then decided to enter Arizona State."

As a freshman at Arizona State, Charley was ticketed for the end slot again, but during the first week of practice, one of the halfbacks became hurt and Charley was first in line to replace him.

Charley never had a real good relationship with Sun Devil coach Frank Kush, though the two came away with a mutual respect after four years. It was just a matter of personalities. For instance, Kush was the verbal type who liked a lot of noise, a lot of hollering and growling.

Charley, on the other hand, was quiet almost all the time. He didn't go for all the growling and yelling, though it never affected his play.

"For Coach Kush to say a guy's good, a guy's got to chatter a lot," Charley said. "This growling business starts in high school. I'm glad the pros don't get carried away with it. I just never did it. It takes different things for guys to get their momentum up. Mine builds up the morning of a game. If one guy needs to holler all week, fine, let him do it."

Charley also had a lifelong habit of sometimes taking it a little easier in practice. It was his way, and often led people to bum-rap him in those days. A teammate remembers.

"Charley would get downright lackadaisical in practice sometimes and Coach Kush would have to get on him. But I never knew Charley to put out less than his best in a game. Coach knew this. But he couldn't let Charley get away with going through the motions all week. It wouldn't have been a good example for the rest of us, those who had less talent than Charley and needed the work."

Then came another crisis, this one during spring practice before Charley's sophomore year.

"I was playing defensive back and I came up to make a tackle on the ballcarrier," Charley recalls. "I thought we were going to hit head-to-head but he lowered his head at the last second and my momentum carried me over his back. It was a rainy day and my helmet stuck in the mud a bit before I flipped over on my back.

"I thought I had pinched a neck nerve because I started quivering and could not stop it. The coach started screaming at me to get up. He didn't know, and I don't blame him for doing what he did. He was tough, like Lombardi, but a good man.

"Anyway, I knew something was wrong because I had to keep pushing my head up straight; it kept falling toward my shoulder. I stayed in for a couple of more plays, then walked off. I lay on the sideline for a half hour or so, then they took me to the infirmary. I could have died if we waited any longer. I had four fractured vertebrae. There was no operation, but I wore a cast for six months. When it came off, my neck was no thicker than one of my forearms.

"But I was lucky. The vertebrae had healed even stronger than they were before and the doctor said I could play football again. Once again my parents were against it, but we talked and I convinced them I had to try."

Coming back wasn't hard, but the first contact drills were frightening, and Charley experienced the same kind of fear that all athletes feel when coming off a serious injury. There's always a lingering doubt that the injury will recur, and when it involves a broken neck, the fear is all the worse.

"Nothing hurt the first time," Charley recalls, "but the third time my neck did hurt a little. I stayed with it, though, and it stopped hurting. After that, I put it out of my mind forever."

During his last two seasons there were no physical problems. Charley was 6-3 and 205 pounds by then, and a good, slashing runner, who could also catch passes coming out of the backfield, and often did double-duty as a defensive back. On offense, he was teamed with another outstanding runner, Tony Lorick, who was a bit shorter than Charley and weighed about the same. Charley's nickname was "C.T." while Lorick was called "Bull." Lorick was also Kush's favorite since he was more of a power back, and the offense was often designed for him.

"When Tony had a good day I felt sort of left out," Charley remembers, "and when I had one it was the other way around. We were good friends, but we always tried to be better than one another."

Both were fine backs, but Charley was telling the truth about the offense. Many of the running plays were designed to move right with Lorick carrying. Charley mostly carried to the left, and had to do much of it by himself, but he didn't complain.

During their senior year of 1963, Taylor and Lorick carried the bulk of the Sun Devil offense as the team won eight of nine games. Lorick carried 105 times for 735 yards while Charley toted 88 times for 600 yards. Lorick scored nine TD's, while Charley crossed the goal line eight times. Both averaged more than 30 yards a runback on kick returns. Lorick also led the team with four interceptions, while Charley was the second leading pass receiver with 11 catches for 217 yards and a 19.7 average. When the season ended, both backs were considered prime pro material, and it was a tossup as to which one was the better pro prospect.

When the draft rolled around Charley became the number one choice of the Washington Redskins, while Lorick was picked on the second round by the Baltimore Colts. In the AFL, the choices were reversed, Lorick being picked first by the Oakland Raiders and Charley on the second round by the Houston Oilers. Both players wound up signing with the NFL clubs.

"I always knew I wanted to play in the National Football League because I thought it had greater prestige," said Charley. "I think I'll be able to help the Redskins. I've seen films of some of their games and it seemed to me that something was missing. I feel I can contribute the most at running back, but I just want to play, and if they want me to play defense, well, that's fine with me, too."

Charley was an honorable mention All-America when he left Arizona State. That left him somewhat short of honors compared to some others, but he didn't care. He would be getting his chance. He played well in several post-season all-star games, included the All-America game at Buffalo, in which he played mostly defense. Then he was ready to go to Chicago for the College All-Star game. This was the first big one of his career.

"The Bears are World Champions and I feel tense," he said. "I feel as if I'm going into a Championship game and I plan to do my best."

But shortly after arriving at the All-Star camp, Charley ran into problems with the Stars' coach, the temperamental Otto Graham. And it all went back to Charley's old habit of taking things easy in practice.

"Charley Taylor is a great athlete, but he's very lazy," Graham told the press one day without warning. "He could have a great future in pro ball or fall flat on his face. It's up to him. But he's been coming late to practice and is the first to leave. It's happened too often for him to be a victim of circumstance. He seems to have no interest. I don't know whether to play him on offense or defense, but I'll tell you something. He's the best athlete in camp, but as of now he hasn't earned the right to start."

The charge opened a whole new can of worms. Redskin coach Bill McPeak didn't like seeing his top choice blasted like that in the press. McPeak wrote a letter to Graham expressing his disgust with the situation. Even Frank Kush, Charley's coach from Arizona State was incensed, and no one knew about Charley's ways better than Kush

"I had Taylor for four years," said Kush, "and he was never late and never missed practice. How many athletes can come back from a broken neck and play again? Graham just doesn't understand Charley. He's a shy kid, almost to the point of being an introvert."

McPeak was equally as vociferous. "Graham is putting a mark on Charley even before he begins his pro career," said McPeak. "We scouted him thoroughly and all our reports have been good. Heck, he played both offense and defense in the All-America game and played on every other unit. He played his heart out and played well. How much more could he do?"

As usual, Charley kept silent. He would let his playing do the talking for him. And as usual, the pros won the game, the Bears taking a 28–17 victory. But had it not been for the play of Charley Taylor, the game would have been more one-sided than that.

Charley caught one touchdown pass from quarterback George Mira, then actually threw for a touchdown on an option pass. He also set up a field goal with a great catch deep in Bears territory. So he had a hand in all of the Stars' scoring.

And that wasn't all. He averaged better than five yards a rush, converted a Mira fumble into a TD when he scooped up the ball and threw his option pass, recovered two other fumbles, and ran back a kickoff 17 yards. It was obvious to everyone that he was the most outstanding all-star on the field. And for his efforts he was named the Stars' Most Valuable Player.

Reporters gathered around asking questions,

hoping Charley would have a few choice words for Coach Graham. Instead, Charley just grinned, "The coach congratulated me on playing a fine game."

As for Graham, all he could say was that "Charley has a brilliant future if he works hard."

So it was on to the Skins, all Graham's charges wiped out by one brilliant performance.

The Redskins were an old NFL franchise, one that had seen some glory years in the 1940's, but had fallen on hard times. The club hadn't had a winning season since 1955. There were some fine individual stars, such as Sonny Jurgensen and Bobby Mitchell, but not enough of them or enough depth to really put together a complete season.

There had to be a place for a fine rookie like Charley and it didn't take Coach McPeak long to find it. He installed the youngster at the running back position and Charley took it from there.

It's an unusual rookie who can star right from the first without making too many mistakes, but Charley Taylor did it. Jurgensen didn't hesitate to give the ball to his rookie runner, and often called his number on pass plays out of the backfield.

Opposing teams had to watch Charley right away. The Skins didn't have much of a running attack before, and Charley had to carry a big burden. In addition, his passcatching ability made him a dual threat. When the Skins whipped the St. Louis Cards in an exhibition game, Charley really showed his stuff. Later, the two clubs met in regular season play and St. Louis won. One of the reasons was an adjustment in the team defense.

"We worked at stopping Taylor," said Card Coach Wally Lemm. "We didn't worry about him in the pre-season because he was just a rookie, but we soon learned he was no ordinary rookie. So the next time we were ready."

The Bears were another team that stacked up against Charley. They held him to just 30 yards rushing and nine on four receptions. But in the final minutes he broke off a 24-yard run that led to the winning touchdown.

There were also some games when they didn't contain him, for by midseason he ranked second only to Jim Brown in total yardage among NFL backs. Charley had 398 yards rushing and had caught 26 passes for 355 yards in that department. There were a couple of dropped passes and a fumble here and there, but all in all, he was having an outstanding year. In fact, about that time someone asked Coach McPeak if he'd trade Charley for Green Bay's versatile halfback, Paul Hornung.

"Before the season I would have made the trade in a minute," said McPeak. "But now there's no way I'd do it."

As the season waned, it was obvious that Charley was a prime candidate for Rookie of the Year. His competition included a teammate, safetyman Paul Krause, Cleveland flanker Paul Warfield, and Tony Lorick, his former Arizona State teammate who had moved into the starting fullback role with the Colts.

But Charley's pace never slowed. The final game was played against the Colts and the Skins needed to win it for a .500 season. For almost three periods Charley worked against a Baltimore defense that was geared to stop him. They pounded him and gang-tackled him mercilessly. Finally, his knee gave out and he had to leave the ballgame with the score tied, 17–all. But once he was out of there, the Colts just ganged up on quarterback Jurgensen and won the game, 45–17. That's how much Charley had come to mean to the Skins' offense.

Still, it had been a great rookie season. Charley was a workhorse, carrying 199 times for 755 yards and five TD's. That was sixth best in the league. He also caught 53 passes, then a record for a running back, gaining 814 yards and scoring another five TD's. He was Rookie of the Year by a wide margin, beating Krause and Warfield, both of whom were fine first-year players.

Everyone had good things to say about him, including his teammate, Bobby Mitchell.

"As far as I'm concerned," said Mitchell, "Charley is the best to come along since Jim Brown. You just don't find the combination of talents he has. He had quickness, speed and strength. Having all three in one player is just too much to ask for. Such a player can't miss being great."

Even bigger things were predicted for Charley in

1965, but the old injury bugaboo came back to haunt him. In the very first pre-season game Charley broke an ankle, not a bad break, but enough to put him on the shelf during the entire pre-season. He was given the OK to start after five games, but the ankle was still tender and he didn't have full mobility. The result was seen in his rushing. He wasn't even getting three yards a carry. And he often limped off the field for short periods during the second half of the games. Yet he continued, displaying courage in the face of pain and criticism of the press and fans, neither of whom knew how he was hurting.

"Last year Charley never went down on the first hit. He used to give it that double fake and always get past the first man," said McPeak. "Not this year. He can't quite pull off the fake because he doesn't have the agility and lateral movement."

The season ended with the Skins 6–8 once again. But Charley's stats were down. He ran for just 402 yards on 145 carries, a dismal 2.8 average, and his receptions were also down to 40 for 577 yards. So he waited anxiously for 1966, which would turn out to be the pivotal year of his career.

For one thing, the Skins had a new coach. He was none other than Otto Graham, the man who had criticized him so vocally at the All-Star game. Fortunately, Graham knew he had been wrong and was willing to forget, especially since he now recognized Charley's multiple talents.

Charley started the season at running back, but

before long he found himself moving out of the backfield for passes more often than carrying the ball. And his running still wasn't real sharp, his per carry average around three yards. Still, early in the year he was named one of the NFL's underrated stars, with testimony from some defensive stars.

Cowboy linebacker Lee Roy Jordan, for one, said, "Charley is very hard to tackle. He's got real good balance and a lot of second effort. There are some guys you can hit and wait for them to go down. Not Charley. You try that with him and he'll go, all right, away from you at a fast clip."

And Dallas defensive back Warren Livingston added, "The toughest thing about Charley is that he'll catch a four-yard pass and it will come out 30 yards in the statistics."

But perhaps that was the tipoff, Charley catching a pass. For after several games in the 1966 season, Coach Graham decided to make a bold move.

"Charley's a great athlete," said the coach. "But the more I looked at him, the more I was convinced he would never be a great running back. He doesn't have the temperament; he's too impatient. He wouldn't wait for the pattern of the play to develop. He'd run ahead of the interference on traps, for instance, and the man who was supposed to be trapped would be there waiting for him.

"He also never learned to glide, to run under control. He couldn't force himself to do it. We noticed that his best runs were to the outside, where he just outran people."

So Graham began alternating Charley between running back and wide receiver. The uncertainty upset Charley. Though he continued to play well, his weight dropped from 210 to 195.

"I'd come home from practice and I'd be so upset and worried that I couldn't eat," he said. "There was this big ball of worry on my mind."

The uncertainty would have unnerved anyone. Plus Charley had always dreamed of following in the footsteps of his idol, Jim Brown, who was, of course, a runner par excellence.

The split positions continued, though Charley was catching more and more passes each week. Finally, in the ninth game, Graham made the change permanent. No more uncertainty, but now a new position. Now Charley had to work all over again.

"Being a running back was something I was just gifted with," he said. "Being an end was something I had to learn myself. I was starting from the ground up and had to do extra work. I clowned around less. In fact, I decided not to clown around until I had everything down perfect."

It wasn't an easy conversion. Teammate Bobby Mitchell had done a similar thing some years before and he told about the way it was.

"It's not hard for a good running back to be a good receiver," said Mitchell, "but there are differences. A halfback is used to having the ball going away from him when he comes out of the backfield for a pass. A receiver runs toward the ball most of the time, or the ball comes to him at an angle. Plus there are different coverages. Defensive backs rarely cover a halfback, but they're always on the wide receiver, so your patterns are more complicated and more difficult to execute.

"Let's face it, when you're running back you love that position. If you have the size, the speed, and the elusiveness, it's the premier position. A halfback can run with the ball, he can pass the ball, he can catch the ball. All a receiver can do is catch. And when you're a halfback, you know you'll be involved in the game. A receiver can just hope he's involved in the game."

It was Charley's rushing that began suffering as he worked to learn the new position. In the sixth, seventh, and eighth games of the year he ran for a total of 32 yards . . . while continuing to catch passes. That's when Graham made the final decision. In the ninth game, Charley was a fulltime pass receiver.

And what did he do that day against the Colts? He ran wild, catching eight passes for 111 yards and a touchdown. A week later he showed it was no fluke. Against the tough Cowboys he grabbed 11. And he was enjoying the broken-field running that went with the position, breaking tackles, showing his elusive moves that had all but disappeared from his halfback play. After several weeks as a wide receiver, Charley was near the top of the league in passes caught.

Going into the final game of the year, he was just four passes behind Detroit's Pat Studstill, who was out with an injury.

"Sure, I'd like to win the title," he said. "But if the game is close I can expect to catch a barrel of passes. We've got to win it, first."

What Charley didn't realize was that the Skins had a better chance of winning when he was catching all kinds of passes. So in that final game he caught eight more, giving him 72 for the season. He had caught 54 of those in the final six games when he became a fulltime wide receiver. In effect, Charley Taylor had become an all-pro wide receiver in less than half a season.

Oh, yes, he took the pass catching title with his 72 grabs, accumulating 1,119 yards along the way, good for a 15.5 average and 12 touchdowns. Add his 262 yards rushing and three TD's on the ground, and that made Charley Taylor one of the top yardage producers in the entire league.

One man who was not surprised at Charley's success was teammate Mitchell.

"I knew Charley would be a great receiver. Heck, he was catching all kinds of passes as a runner. Plus he worked and he worried. My wife and I came to expect our phone to ring at any hour of the night. When it did, we'd look at each other. We both knew it was Charley, worried about something else, calling to ask another question or go over our next game, or talk about defenders. He was really working at his job."

Charley's totals were no fluke. The next year he promptly went out and grabbed another 70 passes and another receiving title, garnering 990 yards and nine scores. It was hard to believe he hadn't been a receiver all his life.

Unfortunately, the team was still struggling to escape mediocrity. They had been 7–7 in 1966, then 5–6–3 in '67. The next year the club slipped to 5–9, and injuries played a part in Charley's slip to just 48 catches. Then in 1969 the club made a change, bringing in the great Vince Lombardi as coach. Lombardi brought his own special magic with him. He didn't have championship personnel, but he brought the club home a winner at 7–5–2. They seemed to be building.

Charley showed his courage again. He broke a hand in training camp, yet came back with a cast on his hand and continued to play well. He caught 71 passes for Lombardi in 1969, getting 883 yards and eight scores. Lombardi loved his skills and his attitude.

"Charley is a threat within himself," said the coach. "He is so dedicated that he is willing to make the sacrifice and play the decoy so Jerry Smith and Bob Long (the club's other receivers) can get loose."

Unfortunately for the Redskins, Lombardi's tenure was short. Prior to the 1970 season he was stricken with a fatal illness. Within months, the great coach who had brought so many championships to Green Bay was dead. The entire football world mourned his loss, and the Skins would have to start all over again.

They didn't become winners until 1971, when George Allen took over the club. It was a milestone year for the Redskins and for Charley Taylor. He was given a new multi-year contract calling for some $70,000 a season. Charley and his attorney, Clarence Rogers, were both pleased.

"Charley was not up where he should have been salary wise," said Mr. Rogers. "He is a superstar and that is the kind of contract he has now. He's finally being paid what he's worth and can concentrate on his playing."

Always a shy and withdrawn person, Charley was now becoming more involved in his community. He was actively involved in drug abuse programs, going around to schools and talking to youngsters, counseling them on the harm drugs can do. There was no pay for this work, but Charley gave of his time freely.

"Nobody had to ask me twice," he said. "Anytime I can do anything to help kids I'll help."

On the gridiron, Charley was still a terror, despite the injuries that caused him to miss more playing time. In 1970 a broken collarbone kept him out for four games and his passes fell to 42. In '71, as the Skins made the playoffs for the first time under Allen, Charley was on the shelf for the final eight games and the playoff loss to San Francisco as he sustained another broken ankle. As the 1972 season approached, Charley was 31 years old, a time when many receivers begin to slow down. But he was optimistic.

"I feel as good now as I have since my rookie season," he said. "I have to believe that the injuries are just freak plays which are part of my past. All I want to do now is play and win."

For once Charley was right about the injuries. He has avoided them since 1970 and has re-established himself as one of the premier receivers in football. He came back with 49 catches in 1972 as the Skins had an 11–3 season and went all the way to the Super Bowl before losing to undefeated Miami, 14–7.

Charley continued his fine, injury-free play in '73 and '74. Despite advancing age he forged into third place on the all-time receiving list with 113 grabs over the two seasons. And there are still very few signs of his slipping.

And now Charley plays a more important role than ever with the Skins. He's offensive captain and takes his job very seriously.

"As a team leader, I have to worry about the whole game now, and not just myself," he said, early in the 1974 season. "To be a captain, you have to have the respect of the coaches and maintain the respect of the players as well. You must give 120 percent all the time. You can never get depressed, and when you see others that way, you have to pick them up."

So Charley Taylor has come a long way from the shy, introverted rookie who was accused of being lazy at the College All-Star game more than a decade ago. And he's come a long way from the talented youngster who didn't know from one day to the next whether he'd be a running back or passcatcher.

Well, he's all passcatcher now, and one of the best. And he still plans to get some more mileage from his lean, lithe body.

"When I walk away from the game," Charley Taylor has said, "I want to know that there was something I contributed to football."

Charley Taylor has already made that contribution. And he continues to make it every time he steps onto the gridiron.

Otis Taylor

Otis Taylor is an artist. Anyone watching the tall, graceful wide receiver of the Kansas City Chiefs would have to agree. He brings a kind of flowing, floating, electricity to the game of football. Unlike some receivers who pursue their profession with a kind of clinical precision, Otis frequently free-lances, sprinting through his patterns and gathering in passes with a fluid ease that often leaves defenders gasping and frustrated in his wake.

The 6-3, 215-pound Taylor has been doing it at an all-pro level for more than 10 years now. There've been times when people have said he was on the way down, that his skills were diminishing. But just as some of the fans were beginning to believe it, there'd be Otis, making another one of his amazing catches, sometimes in a crowd, then sprinting away for another long score.

Some of his pass-run plays are classic. It was his 46-yard score in the 1970 Super Bowl that put the game out of reach of the Minnesota Vikings. On that play, Otis took a pass from quarterback Len Dawson on the right sideline. Defensive back Earsell Mackbee rushed up to blast Otis out of bound. But Otis was ready. He did a quick stutter-step, then pushed Mackbee aside with his free arm and accelerated down the sideline. When another Vike tried to angle him out, Otis cut back to the inside, straight-armed him, and sprinted into the end zone.

Then there was a big game against Washington in 1971. Otis was working the right side against a superb defensive back, Pat Fischer. As usual, quarterback Dawson looked for his favorite target. He fired high. Since Otis was several inches taller than Fischer, the wily defender managed to pin Otis' left arm to his body, making it virtually useless for the catch. But as the ball came down, Otis reached up with his right arm, pulled the ball into his body with a swift, graceful cradling motion, then left Fischer sprawled in the dirt as he ran for the score.

There are endless examples of Otis' skills. He himself admits that many of them come naturally. For instance, there was one year when K.C. took a chance on a former Olympic sprint champ, hoping to make him a wide receiver and utilize the man's burning speed. Coach Hank Stram asked Otis to work with the youngster, and he did, giving his time and advice freely and often. The experiment failed, and when it did, Otis talked about it and about the art of catching passes.

"We were making some progress," said Otis. "But people were trying to teach him something I don't think can be taught. You can't teach a person the catching ability, the running ability, the grace.

"There's a fine art about catching. I think it must be some ability, some feel, that a person has. I don't think this man had this feel, although he was getting better before he was cut.

"So much of it is instinctive. If someone woke me up in the middle of the night and threw a football at me, I'd catch it."

Otis wasn't playing games or boasting. He was telling it like it is. He's always been a candid, an honest man, whether evaluating himself or other gridders, or talking about outside opportunities for black athletes, a subject he feels very strongly about. He doesn't think there are enough and has been trying to do something about it. A football player, even an all-pro, can't bask in the glory forever. The time always comes when he must do something else. Otis knows this.

"Sure, I make good money in football," he said, "but it can eat you up to see the white ballplayers getting all kinds of feedback and you getting nothing. Sometimes I just sit up at night and think, 'What am I going to do with my life when this is all over?' It can be a very frightening proposition."

But Otis Taylor has faced frightening propositions before. He was forced to grow up, forced to make decisions, and has always come out on top.

Otis Taylor, Jr., was born on August 11, 1942, in Houston, Texas. He had just one sister, but both his parents had to work very hard just to make ends meet. His mother, however, was a strong, forceful woman who always watched out for her children and tried to make sure they had everything they wanted.

"My mother always gave us nice clothes and shoes, and the other things we needed. She and my father both worked very hard. Whenever there was something we needed, my mother found a way to get it for us. In that respect, we were never poor."

Otis began playing ball early, like so many future athletes, and he played all the sports, as often as he could. Of course, there were days when he didn't come out on top and wasn't in very good shape when he got home that night. His mother took care of that, too.

"Boy, she used to tan my hide," says Otis, with a grin. "If I came home with a bloody nose or torn clothing, I got it good."

It didn't stop Otis from playing ball. No way anything would do that. He says now that he never wanted to be anything but a professional athlete.

The only problem was picking the right sport, and he was good at all of them. There was basketball, baseball, football, and even track. At one time or another he favored each one.

First it was baseball. Then, when Otis reached Worthing High School in Houston, basketball took over.

"That's when I saw Elgin Baylor play for the first time," Otis recalls. "I just fell in love with the way that man played the game. He was so great. I tried to imitate everything he did on the court, all those fantastic moves. My problem was I couldn't shoot all that well. But by devoting all that time to basketball, I think I became quicker and more agile in football."

Don't get Otis wrong. He was a pretty good ballplayer. He averaged about 17 points a game in high school and had one Baylor-like night when he poured in 41.

Then there was track. Otis was a sprinter, a long jumper, and high jumper. But he never really took to the sport.

"Track is a punishing sport, and you're all by yourself out there. No one can help. I could do a 9.7 hundred and they said I'd get better. But I didn't care. I didn't really like track anymore and didn't want to pursue it.

"To tell the truth, I had no real goals set then and didn't have any idea what I'd do or how things would come out. I suppose it could have come out a lot worse."

Then there was football. Otis was a quarterback at Worthing and a good one. His size and grace impressed the local college scouts, though not too many of the big-timers came around. Still, he made all-state as a senior and was offered a full scholarship to Prairie View A & M, an all black school located some 50 miles north of Houston.

So Otis went there as a quarterback, much like another great wide receiver, Gene Washington. And, like Washington, it didn't take long for a change of positions.

In Otis' case it happened at the beginning of his sophomore year. Some of the coaches began watching him horsing around before practice. They kept noticing the ease with which he caught the ball, the way he strided out, reached up, and pulled it in, as if there was glue on his hands. It happened day after day. Plus they could see that the youngster liked catching, almost more than throwing, so it seemed. He certainly had the height, reach, and speed to be an end.

The coaches looked at the rest of their squad. There were a couple of other quarterback prospects who might do the job as well as Otis, but no other receivers with the same kind of potential that the big soph had. They asked Otis if he wanted to become a wide receiver and he gave them a quick YES!

In one of sports' many coincidences, the new Prairie View quarterback was Jim Kearney. He, too, would later change positions, becoming a top strong safety on, of all teams, the Kansas City Chiefs! But at Prairie View he remained a strong-armed quarterback who soon found a favorite receiver in Otis Taylor.

The two players formed a devastating combination for three seasons. Otis would wander all over the opposing team's secondary and Kearney would find him. Their long passing plays became the scourge of the conference. Kearney just had to pop it out there and more often than not Otis would get it, making his own patented, graceful catches, often pulling the ball in one-handed. It was as if he'd been a receiver all his life.

In three years the two combined on some 42 touchdown passes. Otis was especially effective his senior year of 1964. He was an NAIA small college all-America and had scouts from both the NFL and AFL drooling. Both leagues wanted him.

It was still pre-merger days and the two leagues competed for the available talent, trying everything to lure the big-name players into their respective folds. There were some practices that were downright underhanded, and the Otis Taylor case was a prime example.

Otis was still a happy-go-lucky youngster in those days. Football was a joy. He knew nothing of the dog-eat-dog battle the pros went through to get talent. To him, college ball was a fun and exciting time.

"I loved catching Jim's passes for three years,"

he said. "But I did have one problem as a receiver then. I also loved to run with the ball once I got it, and I was often so anxious to run that I'd forget about making the catch and concentrate on running. The result was more dropped passes than I would have liked. You see, I just didn't like settling for just a catch. I'd jump, skip, dance sideways, or do anything to get the ball a little further upfield. It wasn't until one of my coaches convinced me to 'look' the ball into my hands that I stopped dropping them."

Otis figured he'd be the man running with the ball when it came to choosing a pro team. He wasn't prepared for the smothering job the pro boys could do. The two teams competing for Otis' talents were the Dallas Cowboys of the NFL and Kansas City of the AFL.

The whole thing started the Wednesday before Thanksgiving. That's when a Cowboy representative "invited" Otis to Dallas for a little fling. Otis and some other players all converged on Dallas, where they were wined and dined, and taken from one hotel to another.

But there was a method in this madness. It was called "baby-sitting" by some, and "kidnapping" by others. But the trick was to keep the players busy and moving until they signed. That way, representatives from the other league couldn't even find them, much less talk to them about signing a contract.

Otis remembers: "We went from one hotel to

another, moving about three or four times. And it was first class, all the way. I never thought of it as kidnapping. Heck, they didn't have any handcuffs on me. I stayed because I wanted to. It was exciting to be young and so wanted."

Now the plot thickens. A K.C. representative named Lloyd Wells began searching for Otis. He knew what was happening. He also had been following Otis since junior high and wanted to get him on the Chiefs. For three days Wells scoured the Dallas area with no luck. Then he contacted a girl who knew where Otis was staying. He went to the hotel, crept up the back stairs, and confronted Otis.

"What are you going to do, man," he asked. "Are you going to sign with them or give us a chance?"

"I don't know," said Otis, who had already received all kinds of promises from the Dallas club.

"You've *got* to know," said Wells. "You're the man who has to make up his mind . . . and soon."

Then Wells began talking Kansas City, about the future Otis would have there.

"I began to realize the fun was over," said Otis. "I had gone into this thing as a boy on a roller coaster. Now I realized I had to grow up fast and make a man's decision."

So it was down the back stairs with Wells and onto a plane to Kansas City, where there was some good solid talk and no parties. That's when Otis decided. He'd sign with the Chiefs. The deal was a new car, a $10,000 bonus, and a first-year salary of $14,000. It wasn't the same kind of contract some of the big boys got, but it was more than Otis had ever dreamed of before. Now, he was a pro.

The Chiefs were an American Football League original, starting with the league in 1960, although the franchise originated in Dallas as the Texans. In 1962, the Texans won the AFL title by beating the Houston Oilers, 20–17, in an epic, sudden-death battle. Then, in '63, the club slipped to 5–7–2 and finished at 7–7 in '64. But they were beginning to get a nucleus of good, young players and the future looked bright. Coach Stram was looking forward to 1965 and was ready to run a tough training camp. The whole thing had Otis awed.

"Some rookies are real cocky," he said. "They come in figuring they've got it made. Some do, some don't. But it was a completely foreign experience for me and I was scared. In fact, I was scared right up to the last cut."

But after the last cut, Otis was still there. The coaches could see the potential. His natural abilities and assets just hit you smack in the face. Only a dunce could overlook them.

The Chiefs' best receiver in those days was a man named Chris Burford. He wasn't at all like Otis in that he was one of those clinical receivers, not very fast, but one who perfected his moves and had a sure pair of hands. If he could reach it, he'd catch it. Stram asked Burford to help the rookie and at first, Otis misunderstood his intentions.

"I'd go out on a pass and maybe mess it up," recalls Otis. "Chris would call me out and tell me what I'd done wrong. I didn't know how to take it. I was suspicious. 'Man,' I thought, 'why is this cat trying to put me down?' It seemed he was always calling me out. Finally it dawned on me what he was doing. 'Otis,' I thought, 'this man is trying to help you.' That's when I began listening and I can't tell you how much of a help Chris was. I'll never forget him for that."

But when the 1965 season opened Otis was watching Burford and Frank Jackson work the wide receiver slots. He was relegated to the special teams and quickly showed he wasn't afraid to stick his head in and put his body on the line. The coaches liked that. And whenever Burford or Jackson needed a breather, Otis got into the ballgames. He began to learn about the way pro defensive backs operate.

"I came in fully expecting some intimidation from the cornerbacks and safeties," Otis said. "But I really didn't expect everything I got. It was a lot rougher than I thought. They did a lot of bumping and tried a lot of little things to trick me."

But Otis wasn't intimidated for a very long time. He soon formulated his own personal philosophy that would carry him right to stardom.

"I figured it this way," he said. "When the ball

is up in the air, it's mine as much as it is yours. And I'll go after it and use my body to get it."

And when you're 6-3, 215 pounds, fast and graceful, there are a lot of ways to get the football. Week after week Otis showed improvement. Even during his short stints at receiver, quarterback Dawson went to him when the situation called for it. After 11 games, Otis had grabbed 10 passes for 208 yards and a pair of scores. His 20.8 per catch average was by far the best on the team. His potential as a deep threat was clearly visible, and his presence in the lineup gave the Chiefs' offense an entire new dimension.

Then, with three games left to the 1965 season, Burford was injured. It was the perfect opportunity for Coach Stram to test his young receiver full time. Otis began working the outside and Dawson looked his way with increasing frequency. Over those final three games the rookie began to come on. He grabbed 16 passes for another 238 yards and three more TD's. That gave him a rookie log of 26 catches for 446 yards, five scores, and a 17.2 average. Just one other rookie receiver, George Sauer of the Jets, did better, and by just three catches. But on the other hand, there were just four receivers in the entire league who had a better per catch average than Otis.

As for the Chiefs, they finished with a 7–5–2 mark in '65, putting them in third place in their division. But the potential was there. The Chiefs had to be regarded as a threat in '66.

It wasn't long into training camp when it became obvious that Otis would be in the starting lineup, playing alongside Burford at wide receiver. In the team's third pre-season game that year he really exploded, grabbing five passes for a whopping 144 yards. And he had a 75-yard touchdown reception called back by a penalty.

Once the season started Otis was just as good. The team was winning and the lanky receiver was driving defenders crazy with his circus catches. Plus he gave the team a constant deep threat which had to be guarded against at all times.

The best team the previous few years in the AFL had been the Buffalo Bills. The Bills won league titles in '64 and '65, and were considered a major threat again in '66. It was against them that Otis played his best. The first time the clubs met he grabbed six passes for 136 yards, and the second time four for 125 yards. He seemed to be the most dangerous when the chips were down, the mark of a superplayer at any position.

Otis continued to catch passes and the Chiefs continued to win. The team had come of age. Both offensive and defensive lines were massive and tough to penetrate. Quarterback Dawson was a classy veteran who now had an all-league runner in Mike Garrett and a potential all-league receiver in Otis. And most of the supportive players were above average. It was a full 40-man squad contributing to the effort, and Otis was one to see it as it was.

"No group of 40 men is all brotherly love," he said, "but I think we are closer than any team in football."

Otis liked that, and the close friendships he formulated during his early years with the club. Yet there were times when he wanted to be alone, especially before a ballgame. Every player has his own way of preparing for combat, and Otis Taylor was no exception.

"The night before a game I've got to be by myself," he said. "I don't usually sleep well at all and I just lay there with the television on and maybe fall asleep around one o'clock and when I wake up in the morning the TV is still on. When I get to the stadium I've got to be alone, even more so. I like to dress slowly, by myself, then just sit in my stall and think things out."

Once the game started Otis pulled out all stops. Though a freelance type of receiver who could improvise off a pattern without thinking, he still wanted to learn the patterns and all the classic moves that make them work.

"I like running all the different patterns during the course of a game," he said. "That way you get the feel of the defender's reaction. You see what you can do against him. Then when you feel you can beat a man with a certain pass route, you tell the quarterback.

"Moves are most important on the sideline patterns, hitches, and post patterns, because that's when you've really got to work to shake the defender. My moves are improving, but it will probably take another three or four years for them to become really good. By then I should have the good sideline moves and all the wrinkles that other top receivers have."

Patterns and moves notwithstanding, Otis was doing something right, something very right. When the season ended the Chiefs had won their division with an 11–2–1 mark, and Otis Taylor had emerged as one of the best receivers in the league. He had grabbed 58 passes for 1,297 yards and a 22.4 average. He also caught eight TD passes from Dawson, the longest being an electrifying 89-yard pass-run play. No one could take the youngster lightly, that is if they didn't want to get burned, burned fast and bad.

The 1966 season was a milestone year for the American Football League. Pre-merger agreements had been signed with the older National League, and although there was no inter-league play as yet, there was a championship game set for the first time. It was to be called the Super Bowl and would match the championship teams from both leagues. So there was a great deal more than usual at stake when the Chiefs took the field against the Eastern Division winner Buffalo Bills for the AFL title.

Even though the Bills were slight favorites, it was obvious from the beginning that the Chiefs had the younger and stronger team. Though the game was played in the frigid Buffalo winter, the

Chiefs began wearing down the Bills in the second quarter.

The opening session had been a stalemate. K.C. scored first on a Dawson to Fred Arbanas pass. Buffalo tied it on a long bomb from Jack Kemp to Elbert Dubenion. Then, in the second period came the turning point of the game, and it involved Otis Taylor.

The Chiefs were driving again and quarterback Dawson hit Otis with a bullet down the middle that the big receiver grabbed on the 10-yard-line of the Bills. He grabbed the ball with two Buffalo defenders, Tom Janik and Butch Byrd closing in.

Janik hit Otis first, but hit him high, and to the amazement of the fans bounced off Taylor and sank to the ground. Otis kept his feet and spun around, but as soon as he took a step forward he ran into Byrd, a big, tough back who liked contact. The collision was a brutal one and both men recoiled. But it was Otis who recovered first, plowed forward again, and this time ran right over Byrd and into the end zone. The play seemed to take the starch out of the Bills and paved the way for a 31–7 Kansas City win. The Chiefs were AFL champs and headed for the Super Bowl. And after the game, most of the talk was about Taylor.

"Taylor can intimidate you," said the veteran Byrd, who had met up with the best during his career.

Patriot coach Mike Holovak was even more complimentary. His club had been victimized by one of Otis' one-handed grabs during the season, a catch Holovak called "out of this world." And after the Buffalo game the coach compared Otis with the league's premier receiver, Lance Alworth.

"The only difference between Taylor and Alworth," said Holovak, "is that Taylor is bigger. If I had to pick between them I'd flip a coin."

And Hank Stram wouldn't even bother with the coin. "Otis is the most complete wide receiver in the league," he said, "because he has speed, sure hands, and can block like a tight end."

Otis himself chuckled about all the fuss his TD had made. "Heck, if it had been a warm day in Buffalo I'd have been knocked out," he said. "It was so cold that I stayed conscious. But I was really out of it for a little while. I didn't know where I was going or who I was bumping into. When I look at the pictures of that play it doesn't surprise me that I scored. But it scares me. I still shake my head."

There'd be some more headshaking by the whole K.C. team. For they had to meet the powerful Green Bay Packers in the first Super Bowl game. The Pack was heavily favored and considered one of the greatest teams in football history. When Green Bay scored first it looked like it might be a rout. But the Chiefs showed their grit and came back with 10 second quarter points. At the half, Green Bay led, 14–10.

Then came the turning point. The Chiefs were driving in the third period when Willie Wood intercepted and ran all the way to the K.C. five. The resultant TD made it 21–10 and Green Bay took over to win, 35–10. But the Chiefs had held their own.

Otis wasn't a big factor in the Super Bowl, though he caught four passes and impressed most NFL observers. But over the next few years he solidified his reputation as one of the best receivers in the game.

He caught 59 passes for 958 yards the next year, scoring 11 touchdowns. In 1968 he was injured part of the time and limited to 20 catches. Yet he gained 420 yards on those for a 21.0 yard average. The Chiefs were a different team when Otis was in there. As Coach Stram said:

"We used to travel by bus. With Otis, we go by jet."

The problem was that in '67 and '68 the Chiefs were playing well, but playing second fiddle to the Oakland Raiders in the Western Division. In fact, in 1968, both the Chiefs and Raiders had identical 12–2 records in the regular season, but the Raiders won the playoff game in a romp, 41–6. So when 1969 rolled around, the Chiefs wanted to get back that divisional championship. They wanted it bad.

Otis, too, wanted to win, and he wanted to stay healthy after his injury-plagued year of 1968. There was also another mouth to feed. Otis married in June of 1969. He had known his wife, Cheryl, at Prairie View, but they didn't begin dating until

1966. So Otis came to camp anxious to start, and Hank Stram was one person who was glad to see him.

"Otis can run, catch the ball, block, and run reverses, which slows up pursuit and helps the rest of our game," said the coach. "He has continued to develop. Last year he was off to a great start but an injury prevented him from expressing all his ability. But everyone on the team respects his skills and the contributions he can make to our success."

The skills were all there in '69, though minor injuries limited his movement in several games. He still managed 41 receptions for 696 yards and seven scores. The Chiefs had a good season, finishing at 11–3. The only problem was the Oakland Raiders had a brilliant season and a 12–1–1 record. This put K.C. second again. Only this time there was a change in the playoff system, a one-year change to accommodate the NFL, with whom total merger was a year away. So the second place teams had a shot at the title.

It worked out well. The Chiefs were ready for a big effort and whipped the defending world champ New York Jets, then topped Oakland, 17–7, for the league crown. For the first time in history a second-place team was going to the Super Bowl. This time the Chiefs would be meeting the powerful Minnesota Vikings of the NFL.

The Vikings were a traditional straight-ahead team, with a rather plodding offense and superior defense. Yet they were heavy favorites. What they weren't ready for was the confusing, multiple offense of the Chiefs. K.C. took a 16–0 halftime lead on three Jan Stenerud field goals and a TD drive.

Then the Vikes scored early in the third period. It looked like the momentum was changing. That's when Otis took over, grabbing a short sideline pass from Dawson, putting his brilliant move on Earsall Mackbee, then racing 46 yards for the clinching score. The defense took charge after that and the final was 23–7. The Kansas City Chiefs were world champs and for once the entire football world got to appreciate the talents of Otis Taylor.

In 1970 the Chiefs dropped back to second, and Otis fought the injuries again. He nailed just 34 passes for 618 yards and there was some talk around the league about him slowing down. He just laughed. "Maybe I'm not quite as fast as when I came up, but I'm not that slow, either. And any loss of speed I make up with experience."

So in 1971 Otis went out and proved it. He was football's outstanding receiver once again, grabbing 57 passes for 1,110 yards, a 19.5 average and seven scores. And the Chiefs regained the divisional title with a 10–3–1 record.

All season long Otis was the main man in the attack. He was the guy they went to in the clutch, and more often than not, he made the key changes, sometimes with two or three defenders hanging all over him.

"When they're going to me in a big situation the guys in the line have the feeling I'll do something with the ball. That makes me feel pretty good and want to get it even more."

After a big win over rival Oakland, quarterback Dawson and Coach Stram echoed those thoughts. Someone asked Dawson if he was picking on a particular cornerback.

"No, I wasn't throwing against a cornerback," said the QB. "I was throwing to Otis. Why not go to our best?"

Said Stram, "It's true that we feel we've got to get the ball to Otis when we need a big play. I just can't describe his catches. I don't know enough adjectives. I don't even know how you press people can describe him."

Though the Chiefs lost in the playoffs, a two-period sudden-death heartbreaker to Miami, it couldn't dampen the great season of Otis Taylor. He was a consensus all-pro for the first time (combined AFC and NFC) and was named the AFC's Player of the Year by United Press International. His salary was comparable to the game's other top players, but there was something missing, and Otis didn't like it. It worried him, and it made him angry.

"I've been around a long time now and I haven't seen the off-field opportunities for black athletes improve at all. I don't normally pop off about it, but I'm not the only athlete affected and I don't like it.

"For example, there are a whole group of white ballplayers on the team who get the use of cars from local dealers. The only black who has one is Willie Lanier, and that's because it's a set thing for the player representative.

"I was called to New York during the off-season to receive an Outstanding Player Award from the Long Island Touchdown Club. Since I was the first receiver to get it I was very proud. But there was a banquet about two miles from my home in Kansas City and I didn't receive anything, not even an honorable mention. It was sickening.

"Sure, I'd like to make Kansas City my permanent home, but I'd also like to have something to do to enable me to take care of my family comfortably when I retire. Heck, I'd even do a dog food commercial if I could get the chance."

Otis had plenty of reason to be bitter, and it might have affected a lesser man in other ways. But it didn't stop Otis from making a USO tour of Far Eastern hospitals during the off-season. While playing golf in the Philippines, Otis heard his caddy talking about a 20-mile trip to work each day, a trip usually taken on foot. Without saying anything, Otis went out and bought the caddy a bicycle. Later, when the tour reached Hawaii, they were greeted by a Kansas City music group playing a date in a Hawaiian nightclub. It was learned that Otis arranged the whole thing and had even paid the group's way to the Islands.

He also enjoyed working with youngsters. Besides talking to them at Kansas City schools, he also helped prepare a special book about his life, a book geared for young children with reading difficulties. The book had a special vocabulary, simple sentences, and many illustrations.

"It's a book of enjoyment," said Otis, "to get children interested in reading. Hopefully, the story of a football player will interest them. Through the book I hope to help children to have a better chance in life than I had when I was coming up. I was concerned because so many kids of eight and nine couldn't read and write at all. They didn't even know simple words. When I go around to the schools and see these kids starting to put things together, I feel I'm helping do something that is meaningful, practical, and useful."

Those aren't the actions of a bitter man, just one who sees things as they are and feels changes must be made. As a football player, he continued to excel. He was 30 years old in the 1972 season, yet caught 57 passes for 821 yards and six scores.

Minor injuries and a general deterioration of the team have contributed to diminished numbers the last two years, 34 and 24 receptions respectively. Part of the problem could be that long-time quarterback Len Dawson has also been injury prone and is nearing the end of the line. He and Otis have worked so well together for so long.

Now the club is rebuilding under a new coach and some trade rumors have been circulating the last two years. Otis will be 33 years old when the

1975 season opens and that's not young for a receiver. Most of them don't last that long. Otis still works hard on the field and has been working hard to put together a future when his playing days end.

Even if his career should end tomorrow Otis Taylor will be remembered as one of the all-time great ones. He has been all of that . . . and more, a graceful receiver, at his best when the chips are down, capable of catching any ball at any time.

Perhaps one of Otis' greatest tributes came in 1972 when he met Don Hutson at a sports banquet. Hutson was a great Green Bay pass-catcher of the 1940's, a Hall of Famer who still holds the record for the most touchdown catches in a career.

When the two men were introduced, Hutson shook Otis' hand and said, simply:

"I've seen you play. You are the greatest!"

Many people around the National Football League would have to agree with that.

Bob Tucker

Looking back at it now, it may all seem like a bad dream. After all, Bob Tucker is widely respected as one of the best pass receivers in football, a tight end who excels in all phases of the game required at that position. But not so long ago, Bob Tucker was experiencing a football nightmare, the nightmare of not getting a chance to show his stuff anywhere in the league.

Some fans may think that cannot happen, that NFL scouts and coaches are so thorough that no stone goes unturned, no talent unnoticed, no player cut without a good look. And if a player is cut for some reason, another team will be ready to scoop him up and get his talent out on a field.

But it doesn't always happen that way, and the Bob Tucker story is a prime example. In fact, just listening to Bob's story makes one wonder if there isn't a team of all-pros sitting by their televisions all across the country each Sunday afternoon in the fall, watching others perform on the gridiron.

It wasn't that Tucker was a late-bloomer, a guy who didn't come into his own until he sat the bench a few years learning his trade from proven veterans. No, that wasn't the problem. It was more a matter of finding the right place at the right time, and overcoming the onus of a small-college career that left Bob Tucker completely out of the pro draft, despite setting records and making the Little all-America teams.

He could have been discouraged right then, but he wasn't. Bob decided to stick with it and play in the so-called minor leagues. As always, the 6-3, 230-pound Tucker was a standout, yet he could get no closer to the NFL than the taxi squads, first with the New England Patriots, then the Philadelphia Eagles.

And when the New York Giants decided to give him a shot prior to the 1970 season, Bob himself admitted it was a now-or-never situation. Had the Giants not given Bob a chance to show his stuff, he probably would have taken his all-pro talents and gone into teaching or perhaps business, undoubtedly meeting with success, but never having the opportunity to show the world what he could do from the tight end slot.

Fortunately, Bob Tucker got his chance. He became a starter after four games and went on to grab 40 passes for 571 yards. He was also a demon blocker, ran well with the ball, and quickly became one of the team's prime offensive weapons. Bob Tucker had it made . . . at last.

When Bob Tucker was a youngster growing up in Hazelton, Pennsylvania, the last thing on his mind was his future struggle to get a chance at playing in the NFL. He was born in Hazelton on June 8, 1945, and was brought up there, right in the heart of Pennsylvania coal mining country. His father was a construction foreman in nearby Wilkes-Barre, and always provided well for the family.

But that didn't mean Bob had a pampered childhood, not in Hazelton. It was a rough place, where the boys played hard no matter what they were doing. And the thing they did the most was football.

"You either played football in Hazelton or they made fun of you," recalls Bob. "It didn't always help me, though. I was a skinny kid and I stayed that way until I got to high school. So I wasn't much good at football and I heard about it from my friends. But their remarks kept me from quitting and I always played, even when I took quite a licking."

But the lickings toughened Bob up. And when he reached high school, he was filling out to a big, strong, handsome lad who could handle himself on the gridiron with anyone. He knew how to use his natural strength and speed, and when necessary his fists.

Bob was a center in high school, doubling as a linebacker on defense, and doing a slam-bang job both ways. He was already at his full height of 6-3, and his weight was climbing rapidly toward the 220 mark. It became obvious early in his senior year that he was college material. The offers didn't flood in, but they came, and Bob soon made his decision.

"I took a scholarship offer from West Texas State University," he said. "Going to Texas seemed like a good idea at the time. They had me at center out there and the football was fine. It was the place that started to get me. I just didn't like it. It was flat and dry country, unlike anything I'd ever seen and I couldn't get used to it, the country or the weather. I started at center as a freshman, but even that didn't help. I was still unhappy. I stuck it out through that freshman year, but that was it. I knew I couldn't go back.

"At first I thought about quitting and just getting a job. But the more I thought it through the more I realized that I had to continue with college because the education would help me more in the future. That's when I decided to go to Bloomsburg State."

Bloomsburg State was a small school located in Pennsylvania near Bob's home. There was a football team and the players took the game seriously, as seriously as at Notre Dame or Ohio State. But there was no realistic way to compare the caliber of play or the competition. Though there were some outstanding gridders, most of the players weren't as big, as strong, or as fast as the heavily recruited high school stars who go to the big football schools. But at this point in his life, Bob really didn't care about those things.

"I felt I was a good football player and could cut it anywhere," Bob recalls, "so it didn't bother me that I was headed for Bloomsburg. In fact, I guess you could say I was pretty cocky when I got there.

"The first day of practice the coach asked me what position I played and I told him I was a center. There were seven other centers already there and I beat them out for the starting job. Then the coach asked me where else I thought I could play. He said that if I played center a lot of other guys would sit the bench, but if I could play another position, at least the second-string center would play. That's when I told him I'd like to be a receiver."

Bob had never played end before, but with his confidence he wasn't worried . . . and neither was the coach. Before long, Bloomsburg had a two-way starter at end, with Bob standing out both offensively and defensively. He was a tough egg, a strong player, one who was willing to stick his head in the meat grinder on defense, and who showed improving skills and class on offense.

So Bob played football and studied hard at Bloomsburg. Playing for a small school in a relatively unknown conference is quite a different experience from the Big Ten, Southwest Conference, or Pacific Eight. There are no huge crowds in mammoth stadiums, no national television audiences, no articles in the big-name sports magazines. In many cases, the games and settings resemble high school contests rather than college encounters.

But that doesn't matter to the players. They play their game just as hard, want to win just as badly, and are susceptible to the same bumps and bruises, and occasionally, the same crippling injuries as the big boys. And the rivalries are just as heated.

"There was one big disappointment each year I played at Bloomsburg," said Bob. "That was we couldn't beat West Chester State. They were our big rivals and they always had good teams, I guess because they're a physical education school. Anyway, one year we played our hearts out and scored 30 points, but still lost."

Bob continued to improve. By his senior year of 1967, he was a bona-fide star. Bloomsburg had put together a good passing game and it was Bob who was usually on the receiving end. The stats began to mount, the numbers were exceptional, but few people notice numbers that are compiled at Bloomsburg State.

There was no real notice outside of the immediate area when Bob set an NAIA small college record by gaining 248 yards receiving in a single game. And there was little notice when he kept catching basketfuls of passes week after week. When the season ended, Bob Tucker had set a couple of more NAIA records by catching 81 passes for 1,325 yards. The recognition finally came, in the form of first-team all-conference and little all-America selections.

Ironically, Bob was only a second team all-Pennsylvania tight end. The first team representative was Ted Kwalick, who played the position with nationally ranked Penn State University. Not that Kwalick wasn't a top performer. Bob would find that out later, when they were competitive rivals in the pros.

At any rate, Bob's college career was coming to an end. He was on his way to a degree in biology with the expectation of starting a career in teaching. Only the pull of the gridiron was still there. Bob began to think about the upcoming pro draft.

"I had heard about NFL scouting systems, about how they managed to feret out prospects from Notre Dame all the way to Podunk. I had had a pretty good season and I figured someone must have seen me, or heard about me. Maybe I wouldn't be a high choice, but I figured I'd go somewhere. And I was beginning to think I'd like to take a crack at it after all."

So Bob waited by the phone as the pros went to

work picking their rookies for the 1968 season. He waited . . . and waited . . . and waited.

"I wasn't drafted," he says. "It was as simple as that. No one wanted me and I thought I should have been picked. Heck, I was aware that Bloomsburg wasn't USC, but the pros are supposed to find people, even kickers in Europe. I just assumed someone would have seen me. It was a big disappointment, but it only made me mad and more determined. I began writing letters and making phone calls. Finally the Patriots—they were the Boston Patriots then—invited me to their camp for a tryout."

If it was a simple fairytale it would have had an immediate happy ending. Tucker tries out; Tucker impresses; Tucker makes the team; Tucker becomes a star. But it didn't happen that way.

"I thought I held my own pretty well in their camp, but I was cut anyway. They still wanted to keep an eye on me and asked me to play for their farm team in Lowell, Mass. So I got a job in the area teaching biology, practiced evenings with the Lowell team, then played in the games on the weekends."

When Bob began working out with the Lowell team he had a rude awakening. He had figured football was football when he played at Bloomsburg, but now he realized that there were some things you just couldn't learn at a small school.

"Nope, I didn't really know that much about the art of passcatching, despite all those balls I grabbed in college. At Lowell, I learned many of the things I'd need later. The coach there was Ross O'Hanlon, who had been a defensive back with the Patriots. He did a good job with the ballclub and gave me my first real experience looking at different offensive and defensive set-ups. I began reading defenses better and learning when to continue my set pass route and when to free-lance off it. No doubt about it, Lowell was a fine football education for me."

Now don't get Bob Tucker wrong. Sure, he was learning, but he was also talented. Despite the inexperience, he emerged as the league's top receiver, grabbing 76 passes in just eight games. Bob figured his performance earned him another shot with the Patriots and this time he figured he'd make it.

"In 1968, Mike Holovak was the Patriots' coach," said Bob, "and he was the guy who promised me a good shot if I played well at Lowell. But you know my luck. I'm reading the papers shortly after the season ended and I see that Holovak has been fired. I jumped to the phone and called the club with a 'what about me' line. I quickly learned that the promise of a contract was no longer there. They told me there were eight or nine tight ends coming in and they no longer needed me. At about that time the Lowell team folded. There I was, coming off a good year, a year in which I worked my tail off, and I had no place to go."

The easy thing would have been for Bob to quit, pack it in, return to his home and another teaching job. But he isn't that kind of guy. More than ever, he felt he could play pro football and he wanted to prove it. He began with the letters and phone calls all over again. This time he got himself a try-out with the Philadelphia Eagles. So with his usual optimism boiling over again, he set out for the City of Brotherly Love.

Bob was a regular dynamo in camp. He was a 6-3, 230-pounder by now and knew how to throw his weight around. Witnesses say he was as impressive as any of the other tight ends in camp. The problem was that the Eagle coaches wouldn't gamble, wouldn't take a chance on the guy from Bloomsburg. They didn't cut him, but they demoted him to their taxi squad and asked him to play with the Pottstown Firebirds of the Atlantic Coast League.

It was a big difference from his experience at Lowell. He was on the Eagles payroll and actually practiced with the team during the week. But on weekends he did his thing for Pottstown, and did it well.

Then came another shock. It seems that the Eagles had a couple of extra players on their taxi squad than NFL regulations permitted. Somewhere around midseason a wiseguy sportswriter blew the whistle. The Eagles were told they had to drop two men from their taxi squad. Guess who was one of them?

"It was a real bombshell. I was right in the middle of practicing, had my uniform on and all. Then this assistant coach comes up to me and tells me I'm cut. Just like that. Man, I mean it almost finished me. I had spent two years sweating and working with nothing to show for it. But I was just sacrificed, in the wrong place at the wrong time. I knew I could play in the NFL. I knew it. I just wanted a chance.

"But I was cut. I was ready to go home all over again. It really took me awhile to get my head on again this time. But I thought it through and realized that football had always been my game and I couldn't quit. Not just yet. So I went back to Pottstown to finish the season there and take one more crack at it in 1970."

Despite the disappointment of being cut, Bob's play at Pottstown continued to be outstanding. Once again he was the league's leading receiver, this time grabbing 66 passes, with a fantastic 17 of them for touchdowns. He was far and away the best receiver in the league. It was hard to believe he couldn't find an NFL team to give him a real look. But he had learned a lot more about playing tight end, and talked about the Atlantic Coast League when it was over.

"It's very competitive in the ACFL," Bob said. "There are good coaches and good players. Let's face it, it's no barroom league. It's a good prep league for a guy like me who didn't get the college training for the pros. A lot of people would be surprised to see the caliber of guys who played there."

Bob's dilemma was now finding another team. Despite his determination to make the grade, he wasn't about to just give his body to the first club that came along.

"I wanted some front money this time," he said. "I knew the score, the summers of eating dirt taught it to me. A free agent from the minor leagues and with a Bloomsburg State background couldn't demand much, but I had to have something for my pocket if I got cut again. Besides, I figured psychologically, that if I cost them something when I went in they'd be apt to give me a better look."

Bob must have been a good salesman. Otherwise, a lot of scouts must have nosed around the Pottstown games during 1969. For a guy who had been treated like dirt by two NFL teams, it was hard to believe that he got himself several offers to choose from before 1970 began.

First there was the Packers. Bob had worked out with the club before the '69 season had ended and when they learned he was free, they offered him a $20,000 pact to sign with them. There were lesser offers from both the Chicago Bears and San Diego Chargers. Then there was the Giants.

They entered the picture when one-time Giant linebacker Tom Scott, who coached in the ACFL, recommended Bob to his former teammate, Giant coach Alex Webster. Webster and his staff looked Bob over while he was starring for Pottstown and decided to come up with an offer. The New York offer amounted to $23,000, including a $5,000 bonus which was Bob's right away. He decided to take it. He also liked the tight end situation in New York, where Aaron Thomas was on the brink of retirement, and the other candidates had about as much experience as he did.

Ironically, the Eagles made one last pitch to get him back, even claiming he was still their property and telling him he had to take their $15,000 offer if he wanted to play anywhere. But Bob was one step ahead of them this time. He had already checked and had his free agent status verified with the Commissioner's office. He was on his way to New York, once again buoyed by optimism, hoping this time would be his time.

For once, Bob got a lucky break. It was the year of the players' strike and none of the vets were in camp. That gave him a chance to see the kind of action he hoped for. It also freed the coaches to spend much of their time with him and the other rookies. Before long it was obvious that Bob Tucker was the best tight end in camp. Plus the rookies got more work than they usually do and Bob was in tip-top shape, in peak form for a maximum effort. This would have to be the year.

The strike ended suddenly, but only four days before a pre-season game with Green Bay. So the coaches had to turn to the vets in order to get their team in shape for the regular season. They wouldn't go very far with a team of rookies. As Bob himself noted:

"I didn't even talk to a coach for a week. They were frantic trying to get ready for the pre-season games it was like all the rookies just died. But I knew I had made an impression over the past weeks and I kept my patience and just waited."

Bob didn't play a whole lot in the early pre-season games. The club wanted to get those vets back in shape and game conditions were invaluable. When he did play, a pass never seemed to come his way. He didn't have a single catch. Then came a game against the Steelers. The team was very flat, and by the fourth period all the subs were in, including Tucker.

"I played the entire period," he recalls, "except when the play called for a pass to the tight end. Thomas would come back in for that one. I was bustin' my neck blocking and he got to catch the passes. But it was worth it, because I was really hitting. I had to. I knew it was my one big chance and if the team hadn't looked so bad, I might not have got even that."

When the game films were reviewed the next Tuesday, several coaches remarked about Tucker's blocking, which had been superb. It made him feel great, and he felt even better when he was told he'd be starting the following week in an exhibition against the Eagles. He couldn't wait.

It quickly became obvious that the coaches finally wanted a real look at Tucker. Quarterback

Fran Tarkenton began throwing to him early, and Bob responded with the greatest day of his young football life.

He was on the receiving end of five Tarkenton passes, carrying two of them into the end zone for touchdowns. Along the way he bowled over several Eagle defenders, using a powerful straight-arm and driving forward for more yardage like a tank. Not only did he make the Eagles eat crow, but he made the Giants believers. This kid could play the game.

"What a difference that game made," Bob said later. "The following week receiver coach Joe Walton began working with me again, on a man to man basis, teaching me little blocking tricks, showing me new things about running my patterns. For the first time I really felt good and could relax at night. Barring injury or something like that, I knew I had it made."

When the season began the Giants were anxious to stabilize and veteran Thomas opened at tight end. A steady, if not spectacular ballplayer, Thomas would keep mistakes to a minimum. With a rookie, even a 25-year-old rookie, you never know. So Bob watched and waited. Somehow, he knew his chance would come.

He saw some action in the first three games, but his enthusiasm was tempered by three straight Giant losses. Then early in the fourth game, against the Eagles, Thomas pulled a hamstring muscle and Tucker was in. He played a fine game, catching a couple of passes and blocking well. The team won. The next week he had his first start and played well against Boston (the other team that had cut him) and the Giants won again. Then came a game against the St. Louis Cards and Bob Tucker really came into his own.

With quarterback Tarkenton throwing Bob's way early and often, the two began connecting. The Cards tried everything, but they couldn't stop the big rookie tight end. Bob gathered in six Tarkenton passes, good for 150 yards and a pair of touchdowns. He was showing speed and power once he had the ball, and his blocking continued to improve. It was now obvious that the tight end job was Bob Tucker's for keeps. Oh, yes, the Giants won again, 35–17.

Another big test came against crosstown rival New York Jets, the first regular season game ever between the two clubs. Once more it was Tarkenton to Tucker. Bob caught three passes, including the big one for the winning touchdown.

"Bob is getting better and better each week," said Coach Webster. "His catching is outstanding already, and his blocking continues to improve. We knew he could do a job on their linebackers and he did."

The Jets always had trouble containing Tucker. Several years later, after Bob had an eight-catch, 104-yard day against them, middle linebacker Al Atkinson talked about defending Tucker.

"It's no mystery. We know what Bob does best,"

said Atkinson. "We watched films of plays when he runs a pattern after blocking first. In that play he blocks, then falls down, then gets up and runs the pattern. We knew he was going to do it but we couldn't stop him. The reason is he does it so well. He'll really stick a guy and wind up on the ground. You see him there and figure no way he can get up and run a pattern. So you leave him. Then there he is, running alone downfield with the ball in his hands. And don't think he's easy to tackle. No way. He's a big, strong guy who knows how to handle himself out there."

Both Bob and the Giants had fine seasons. The club finished at 9–5, its best mark since 1963, and Bob came up with 40 catches for 571 yards, a 14.3 average, and five touchdowns. And he did that after seeing little action in the first three games.

An ankle injury shelved Bob for the first two games of '71. But the job was his, and when he returned it was obvious that he was better than ever, blocking, catching, and running at an all-pro pace.

In fact, Bob played a big role in his first game of the year, catching several key passes in a 21–20 win over St. Louis. When it ended, quarterback Tarkenton talked about how happy he was to have the big guy back.

"Sure there was a difference in our offense this week," Fran said. "The reason was number 38 was back, blocking and catching the ball. That was the difference. Bob is one of the best young receivers I've ever seen. He runs his patterns perfectly, he blocks well, and he's always in there fighting."

As the season continued, it became more and more obvious that Bob was the real thing. Not only did his Giant teammates appreciate him, but the whole league had to take notice. For Bob Tucker was in the running for the NFC's receiving title, an honor that had never before gone to a tight end.

In fact, Bob's biggest rival was another tight end, Ted Kwalick of San Francisco, the same Kwalick who had beaten Bob for the first team berth on the all-Pennsylvania team a few years back. Now both big guys were catching more passes than the fleet wide receivers. Bob had an explanation.

"First of all there's been some injuries to a few of the top wide receivers, guys like Charley Taylor and Dick Gordon. But even more than that has been the influx of new and sophisticated zone defenses that many teams are using. The zones have shut off the long pass to some extent and allowed us tight ends into the picture with up-the-middle stuff."

Of course Bob didn't mention that both he and Kwalick were outstanding football players and they weren't catching passes by default. Fran Tarkenton continued to be the number one Tucker fan as the season waned. It seemed as if Fran the

Scram couldn't say enough about his favorite receiver.

"If Bob isn't an all-pro this year there's no justice in pro ball," said Fran. "He's just got to be the number one tight end around. He never drops the ball, even when they know I'm throwing to him. And he's one of the best blockers I've seen in a long time. On wide plays he never misses his down block, and this year those down blocks have been against people like Carl Eller, Bubba Smith, and Claude Humphrey. They're not easy guys to take out, but Bob does it."

Coach Alex Webster echoed Fran's feelings. Said the coach, "Bob is as good as any tight end in the league. He can do whatever any of them can. He blocks and he's smart and he can catch the ball. He's got great hands and I don't think any other tight end runs with the ball with as much abandon as he does. I mean, he really hurts people."

Of course, Bob felt he could do it all along. But when asked about his sudden success, he didn't spout sour grapes.

"Concentration," he said, simply. "Concentration and hard work are the keys. I think once you establish yourself you have to work twice as hard. The job may be yours when you go to camp, but there are always a bunch of guys after it and that never changes, no matter how good you are or think you are."

Bob Tucker wasn't about to become a fat cat,

despite his success. While he was determined to keep his job, he knew how the guys trying to get it felt.

"I think maybe I can appreciate how the guys on the other side feel," he said. "I came from there, remember. I wasn't a number one choice and didn't get hundreds of thousands of dollars. Ten bucks was always important to me. I think I know the problems real people have. Some guys are kind of isolated, you know, they've been playing football at such a high level it all becomes kind of artificial. They think everybody has steak for dinner every night and drives new cars and spends wads of money. I know how the little guy struggles, because I came from them and I was one of them for a long time."

The memories of those days were forever burned into Bob's mind, and it gave him a kind of hunger that wouldn't go away, no matter how successful he was. But he was the first to admit that the receiving title would be nice.

"Sure, it would mean something to me," he said, "but I'd also like to think I'm helping the team in other ways, doing *all* the things a tight end should do. Blocking, for instance. I've really worked at that. There are times when the tight end is like an extra lineman, and I want to be effective during those times as well."

He was, all right, and he continued catching passes. With just one game left, Bob had 51 catches and Kwalick was right behind with 49. It would be close.

Unlike Bob's rookie year of 1970, the Giants were not contenders in '71. In fact, they were on the losing end of the stick most of the time. And even though the team finished at 4–10, reserve quarterback Randy Johnson and Tucker put on a show in the finale. Bob caught eight passes to win the receiving title with 59 grabs for 791 yards and four scores. In just two years, he was at the top of his game and his profession.

The problem was not everybody believed it. Not only did Bob fail to make all-pro, he wasn't selected to be in the Pro Bowl, either.

"Did it bother me?" Bob repeated a reporter's question about the Pro Bowl. "Would a rap in the mouth bother you? Sure, it bothered me. What else would I have to do to make the Pro Bowl?

"But when I think about it I'm sure there are reasons. First, there's that Bloomsburg State-free agent thing. It's just something you don't shake. Then there's the syndrome about picking the same guys in certain positions year after year. Like centers and tight ends. The guy who made it the year before just has to live and he will get it again. I thought I had a good enough season to play with any all-pro team. But why fight it. I'll just have that much more incentive for this season. Somebody was wrong and I'm going to prove it."

The Giants traded Tarkenton before the '72 season, but it didn't matter to Bob. He continued to catch passes, even though Randy Johnson and Norm Snead were doing the throwing. It didn't take Johnson long to gain all kinds of respect for his tight end.

"They (tight ends) have to be reliable," said Randy J. "They have to be able to block strong and they must have the 'big play' potential. I think that if you run down all the tight ends in the league, Bob has more of each different talent. I'd say he's the best tight end around."

The club finished at 8–6 in '72, with Bob grabbing another 55 passes, second in the NFC to wide receiver Harold Jackson. This time he did make some of the all-pro teams. He was getting recognition at last.

A broken hand kept him out of the exhibition season in '73, but as soon as he came back he was as good as ever. The problem was that the team couldn't do anything right. The rebuilding program and the promise of the year before had just collapsed all around them. Bob was one of the few bright lights in an otherwise disastrous season. In fact, when the Giants were humiliated, 42–0, by the Oakland Raiders, Bob finally exploded.

"We're a bunch of lousy quitters," he fumed. "If we play like this again we wouldn't even be able to be an Atlantic Coast team."

The game also marked the first one in 46 that Bob went without a single reception. Pride in his own performance might have also prompted the outburst. But he was also a team leader now, a veteran, and a man to be listened to. In fact, with Tarkenton gone and halfback Ron Johnson injured and playing below par, many considered Bob the one superstar on the team.

Despite a 2–11–1 mark at the end, Bob still managed 50 catches for 681 yards and five scores. It was a remarkable performance considering the overall team effort. There was no one questioning Bob's status now. His four-year feats could no longer be ignored. In fact, it was harder than ever to picture him being cut by the Patriots and the Eagles. Both those clubs probably find it hard to believe, too.

Most fans couldn't imagine the Giants going any lower than the 2–11–1 of 1973. After all, they had a new head coach in Bill Arnsparger and some new personnel. They also acquired veteran quarterback Craig Morton. But there were too many loose ends, a new system, and an unsettled offense. The result was a 2–12 season in which the offense scored just 195 points.

Bob was also affected by the offensive plunge. He grabbed only 41 passes for 496 yards, the least productive season of his career. But wait a minute! *Only* 41 passes was still better than most receivers in the league. And there were just four tight ends with more. It's just that people have come to take Bob Tucker for granted. They expect more than 50 catches and 700 or so yards.

It's odd, in a way, that people have come to expect so much from Bob Tucker, especially when he had to fight and scrap for two years just to get a chance to prove himself. The unfortunate part of it is that he's now with a team that is struggling to regain respectability. If Bob had played with the Giants during their glory years, everybody would have known him. But no matter what, he'd be the same person. For as he said, he's tasted the other side and he won't forget it. And that kind of hunger keeps a man going.

For Bob Tucker, the incentive will always be there. And that's bad news for the linebackers and safeties who have to cover him. It's not easy, not by any means.

Paul Warfield

Someone once asked Paul Warfield what makes a great football player and this is what he said.

"I think the difference between the great football player and the good football player is the amount of mental preparation the great one gives the game as opposed to the good one. The great athlete thinks about everything. He expects the unexpected. He uses his brain regarding every element of what he's supposed to do. He prepares himself totally for the game coming up. That's the difference."

Paul Warfield is a great football player. There probably aren't five football fans alive who would not agree that Warfield is one of the best wide receivers ever to don a pair of cleats and trot onto the pro gridiron. And he has been a great player ever since his rookie year of 1964 when he joined the Cleveland Browns and caught 52 passes for 920 yards and nine touchdowns.

Prior to the 1975 season Paul Warfield had played the NFL game for 11 years, the first six with Cleveland, the last five with the Miami Dolphins. In that time, he's never been very far from the best, the most feared receiver in the game.

Yet listen to this. During his long career, Paul Warfield never again caught as many passes as he did during his rookie season. And only one time in his long career did he go over the magical 1,000 yard mark for a season, squeaking past with 1,067 in 1968. And Paul Warfield has never once led the NFL in pass receiving!

What that adds up to is simple. Paul just doesn't have the stats that some of the other great ones have compiled. For instance, Lance Alworth, the great wide receiver for the San Diego Chargers, once had seven 1,000-yard seasons in succession. Yet is he considered a better receiver than Warfield? Not by many, though the two are fairly close in ability.

The point is this. A player does not have to always have the big stats to be great. A receiver doesn't have to make a slew of catches to be an all-pro. Paul Warfield is the prime example.

"Remember this," Paul once said when asked about his relatively low numbers of catches, "I've always played for running teams (Cleveland, Miami) and I've never had the ball thrown to me that many times. I never will. I remember when I was in college, a recruiter for the Browns said the club would be throwing my way some 15 times a game.

"Well, it never happened. Not even 12. In fact, the most passes I've ever caught in one game is seven. You put it all together and it comes out to that I've never had the ball thrown to me enough to roll up these huge statistics."

True, but Paul does have one or two statistics working in his favor. During his career he has averaged 20.7 yards a catch. Simple? Well, think about that for a minute. Through 1974, Paul has caught some 371 passes in his lifetime, and each time he grabbed one of those passes, he was averaging nearly 21 yards gained. There isn't another modern receiver who can make that claim.

And despite the lack of thrown balls, Paul has managed to take 77 of those 371 receptions into the end zone for touchdowns. That means about one of every five passes caught resulted in a touchdown! And that's why Paul Warfield is so great, so dangerous. And that's the kind of extra dimension he can give to any good offense. He can make it great.

For Paul Warfield is a perfectionist, a man who worked and worked and worked to be the best possible receiver he could be.

"My objective is to improve each week," Paul

said, early in his career. "I've been working hard on the little things. Receivers can form bad habits and you have to be on the watch for them. You can forget to concentrate completely, or you can start hurrying your patterns. Those are just two things."

Paul Warfield's philosophy never changed. Throughout his career he continued to watch for the little things, to try to improve each week, to attempt to discover new ways of beating defensive backs and the various kinds of double-teams and zones that confronted him. Paul Warfield never let up, not for an instant. Never.

Unlike many other dynamic pass receivers, Paul Warfield is a quiet, even shy individual, one who would hardly be noticed in a crowd. He has described himself as a loner who would rather spend a quiet night home with his family than living it up on the town. Even his size is very average, six-feet, about 185-190 pounds, just big enough not to be one of the little guy like Harold Jackson or Cliff Branch, and too small to rank with big receivers such as Otis Taylor or Harold Carmichael. No, you don't notice him . . . that is, until he's running out under a long pass.

Paul was a quiet, but hard worker from the first. He was born on November 28, 1942, in Warren, Ohio. Warren is in the heart of steel country, and Paul's father worked at one of the mills, a rough job, but one that enabled him to feed and cloth his family without real difficulty.

Young Paul was always smaller than the other boys, but it didn't really bother him, for he quickly found ways to make up for his lack of size.

"As a kid, I could run and jump as fast as anyone in the neighborhood," he said. "Later, I found it was easy for me to become competent in organized athletics."

As in the steel country of Pennsylvania (the area that produced Joe Namath and Bob Tucker, among others) sports and football were very big in the Warren area. Almost every healthy youngster took up the game early, and fans followed the exploits of their local high schools as if the teams played in the NFL.

Although Paul's father was originally from the farm country of Kentucky, he quickly learned about the sports tradition in Warren and enjoyed it as much as anyone else. Though he never pushed his son, Mr. Warfield got young Paul started early with baseball and football, and coached him until the time Paul was old enough for grammar school and little league. Then he let other coaches take over, and while always following Paul's exploits proudly, Mr. Warfield made it his business never to interfere with his son's development.

Paul weighed just 72 pounds when he started playing touch football at the First Street Grammar School. He started as a quarterback, but could hardly throw the ball at all. So they switched him to end, where he seemed to know just what he was doing and already had great speed and coordination.

When Paul reached junior high, the game changed to tackle, and Paul's role quickly changed to occasional observer.

"I weighed about 95 pounds or so my first two years and my mother was afraid they'd run all over me. So she said nothing doing and I stayed away and delivered newspapers."

Then, in his final year at junior high his weight was up to about 110 (to go with his 5-4 height) and his mother gave her permission for him to play. His father remembers.

"Even though he was small, Paul would catch the eye of people as he would run under opponents and was able to throw them off balance. To the boys he played with in Junior High he was a superstar. They thought as long as Paul was in the game, everything would be all right."

Then it was on to Warren Harding High, with no thought of giving up the game. Paul weighed about 145 his sophomore year, but in football-rich Warren, sophomores don't usually see too much game action. It wasn't true of Paul. Early in the season Coach Gene Slaughter motioned toward the bench and into the game trotted Warfield.

It was right out of the storybooks. The first time Paul got his hands on the ball he scampered 60 yards for a touchdown. Paul was a halfback on that play. He was versatile even then, and Coach

Slaughter used him both as a running back and receiver.

The coach was a stern taskmaster, who wanted to win, but more importantly wanted to make better ballplayers and better citizens out of his charges. He wanted them to work hard and he often challenged them.

"If you think you're a better football player today than you were yesterday," Coach Slaughter would say, "go in there and play. If you don't think you're better than you were yesterday, don't go in."

They say there wasn't one time Paul Warfield didn't go in. Since he was working constantly, he knew he must be improving, must be a better ballplayer. He had that kind of confidence, and his coach knew it.

"I've been coaching football for 21 years and I've never seen another player like him," said Slaughter. "Paul believes in himself. He always has. But it's not an ego thing. He's one of those rare players who doesn't compete with other players—he competes with himself."

It was true. The coach remembered many a night when he was closing up his office in the darkness and he looked out on the field to see Paul working by himself, running, sprinting, stretching.

"The thing is," said Coach Slaughter, "that Warfield fits every cliche in athletics. It's scary. Even back in high school you'd look at this kid and find yourself wondering if he was for real."

So Paul was a star for three years at Warren Harding and in his senior year received something like 172 inquiries and 67 formal proposals from colleges and universities all over the country. It was no surprise. The recruiters and scouts knew a good one when they saw him.

The decision wasn't easy, but there were certain factors motivating Paul. He loved his family and home very much and didn't feel like hopping halfway across the country to study and play ball. He'd rather stay close to home, and there were certainly plenty of opportunities within Ohio and surrounding states.

Finally, Paul decided. He would go to Ohio State, one of the best football schools in the land. Since Paul had been used mainly as a halfback in high school, he figured he'd fit with the Buckeye running game, plus a couple of prominent Warren physicians were Ohio State graduates and helped convince Paul the place was right for him.

But just to make sure, Paul went to Coach Slaughter and asked if the coach thought he was good enough for Big Ten football. The coach just laughed:

"That was like asking if the Pope was Catholic," he said, later.

There was just one problem. Paul went to Ohio State, all right, he studied hard, played football and ran track, and he was even an all-America as a senior. But he never really got the chance to display all his exceptional talents to the utmost. That was because Ohio State coach Woody Hayes believed in basic football, the old "three yards and a cloud of dust" theory.

So while the club ran the ball, they generally ran up the middle between the tackles, with the offense calling for big, plodding backs who could grind it out. Paul was too slender to handle that kind of workload and was often shuttled in and out, moved between flanker and halfback. Every so often he'd get a chance to break one, but not nearly as much as backs at schools with wide-open style offenses.

Paul also played defense. He was an outstanding pass defender and good tackler, and chosen all-America as much for his defensive as well as offensive talents. One Big Ten scout talked about the dilemma that faced Warfield at Ohio State.

"Coach Hayes doesn't like a back who ducks and darts all over the place," the man said. "He isn't interested in a home run hitter who can go 90 yards on one play. He wants the back who puts his head down and heads straight for the goal line on an off-tackle play. Warfield isn't big enough to run over people."

Even some of the pro scouts had difficulty evaluating Paul because he never got the chance to really show his stuff. Paul Bixler, player personnel director of the Cleveland Browns, reflects on the problem.

"I saw Paul three times, once in each of his varsity years," recalls Bixler. "In those games he didn't have a chance to do anything outstanding, but I could see the opposition was scared to death of him. They always seemed afraid he'd break away and go for the long one. Several times he got behind the defense but he rarely was thrown the ball. I did like the way he covered his man on defense, so I put him down in our book as a possible defensive back."

With those kinds of problems it would be hard to picture Paul as a number one draft choice since there was so much unseen and unknown about him. Dub Jones, who coached the Browns' receivers, remembers how it happened with Paul.

"About a year or so before the draft a man from Warren, Paul's home town, came down to our camp and sat around talking with us after a workout. He gave us such a brilliant picture of Paul that we couldn't get it out of our minds. All the coaches were there during the conversation. It just stood to reason that if he had it in high school he'd still have it."

If Paul was unhappy at Ohio State he never let on. He wasn't that type of person. He studied hard and worked to improve his game, no matter what kinds of chances he got Saturday afternoons. Even in the spring Paul was dedicated, this time to track. He was a good sprinter (9.6 in the hundred) and an outstanding broad jumper. In fact, one year he competed in the United States-Russian meet and finished third. His best leap ever was 26 feet, two inches, and that's very close to world class.

But football was always Paul's first love and he was overjoyed when he learned he was the number one draft choice of both the Cleveland Browns of the NFL and the Buffalo Bills of the AFL. The year was 1964, before the merger of the two leagues, so Paul would have to decide between the two offers.

"Believe me," Paul recalls, "I had real difficulty studying during the two weeks following the draft. If I signed, I wouldn't be able to go out for track. And that would end any chance of making the 1964 Olympic team. That had been a dream of mine for some time. I also enjoyed baseball and had even thought about a pro baseball career. By signing I'd miss my final baseball season, too.

"But on the other hand being drafted by the Browns was kind of unbelievable. I was from Ohio and had followed them as long as I could remember. Every summer when I was growing up I'd go to their training camp and watch them work out. Jim Brown was my favorite player, naturally, and I had a special feeling for the team. Besides, I wanted to play in the area where I planned to live after my football days were over."

So Paul finally signed, for a rookie salary estimated at about $15,000 per season with a $5,000 bonus. And as soon as he arrived in camp in July of 1964, he began impressing people.

Paul Bixler remembers that the Browns hadn't decided whether to play Warfield on offense or defense when they signed him.

"Our defense needed a boost," recalls Bixler, "and Paul had all the qualifications of a darned good defensive back. But when we took one look at his moves in camp, there was only one answer —the answer to a real need. He was our flanker —period."

And Dub Jones added, "He's the type of boy, from the instant you look at him, see him run, catch a ball, see him fake, see his instincts, you don't have to be a genius to realize you have a natural on your hands. You say to yourself, if he has the other qualities it takes to be a good receiver, then you've got a star in front of you."

The other qualities Jones noted were toughness, the ability to take punishment, and the intelligence to cope with various coverages and situations. Paul soon showed he had all that, too.

In a matter of days, Paul was the talk of training camp, quickly acquiring the "can't miss" label that has jinxed so many rookies before him. But every day his stature grew in the eyes of the veterans and coaches.

"He's great already," said longtime receiver Ray Renfro. "Paul has the finest moves of any rookie receiver I've seen. He's got moves it takes most players at least a year or more to get down. He's got amazing natural ability. He's bigger and faster than I thought he was, and he's also a fine blocker. That's just a bonus, an added plus."

Browns' coach Blanton Collier was a man of

few words. But even he couldn't resist talking about his prize rookie.

"He's one of the rare kind who can make a mistake and still do better than most athletes can without a mistake," said the coach. "For awhile we didn't know whether to put him on offense or defense, but I just felt he had so much potential at flanker that we just couldn't afford to put him on defense."

There was another former Ohio State player in camp, a linebacker named Sam Tidmore. Perhaps he summed up the Paul Warfield story best when he showed absolutely no surprise at Paul's quick success.

"Paul worked on those cuts and patterns every day at Ohio State," he said. "Heck, we had the best passing attack in the country, but Woody Hayes wouldn't use it."

But the Browns would. The Cleveland team had been one of the most successful franchises in NFL history. It had been formed in 1946 in a rival league called the All-America Conference. The Browns promptly won four consecutive ACC championships. Then in 1950, the ACC was absorbed into the National Football League, and critics said the Browns would now be shown up as just a minor league team.

No way. Cleveland dominated the NFL in its very first year, finishing the regular season with a 10–2 mark and whipping the L.A. Rams for the NFL title. From there the team went on to four more consecutive divisional titles and another pair of championships. So from 1946 to 1955, the Browns finished atop their division. They were conference champs again in 1957, but while retaining a winning tradition, hadn't taken a title since. They lost to the Giants by a single game in '63 and figured that 1964 was the year to reclaim it all. And that's where Warfield fit in.

The Browns had a great running attack, what with Jim Brown moving from the fullback spot and the underrated Ernie Green complementing him at halfback. Frank Ryan was a good, though sometimes inconsistent, quarterback. But he had just one topflight receiver in Gary Collins, and Collins was a move man, good on short and medium patterns. He wasn't an outside burner, and without that speed threat, opposing teams were able to double up on Collins. If Warfield made it, everything would open up.

That's just what happened. Paul was a starter in the very first game and immediately began catching passes from quarterback Ryan. His moves were for real, all right, as NFL defenders quickly learned. And when the ball was up there, Paul knew how to go and get it. He even sometimes used his broad jumping ability to help make circus catches.

"Truthfully, I've got to cut down on the jumping unless I'm going up in the air for a high one," Paul said. "When I leap I lose speed and timing. Another thing, sometimes I move too fast for my own good. In a recent game, I faced my guard squarely, then took too many steps before I got moving and fell down. I've got a long way to go in this game."

Many defensive backs wouldn't have agreed. They were already being driven batty by Paul's dazzle. Just when they thought they had him covered, bam, he was gone again. And his halfback experience gave him an added edge after he caught the football. He could go with it and was dangerous from any place on the field. By midseason Paul was among the league's top receivers, the Browns were winning, and he was enjoying the pro game.

"Surprisingly, it's more relaxed here than it was at Ohio State," he said. "In college, the coaches try to fire you up. Here, they don't. They don't want you to get too emotionally charged. Instead, they try to get us ready, mentally and physically. They want us to look forward to the game—to have fun. And it is fun."

It's always more fun when a team is winning and a player is having an outstanding year. When the 1964 season ended, things were just great. The Browns were 10–3–1 and divisional champs. Jim Brown was in his usual spot as the league's top rusher and rookie Paul Warfield had put together a brilliant freshman season.

Paul had grabbed 52 big passes for 920 yards, a 17.7 per catch average, and nine big touchdowns. It was one of the best rookie seasons ever recorded.

And the thrill wasn't over yet. Since there was just one league and two divisions in those days, the playoff system was rather simple. Just one game for the championship. So the Browns met the Baltimore Colts, winners in the west, with a fine 12–2 record. The Colts were slight favorites.

But it was one of those days when things go right for one team and wrong for the other. Cleveland could do no wrong. The Browns took an early lead and just built on it, making the game one of the most one-sided in NFL championship history. Cleveland won it, 27–0, and were once again champions.

Paul caught just one pass in the title game, good for 13 yards. But the Browns really didn't have to throw much. Once they took the lead they were content to let their superb running game do most of the work. It didn't bother Paul. He couldn't imagine a more fulfilling rookie season. Not only was he playing with the one team he really wanted, but he had had a successful year at his position and the club had won the championship. It was a real highpoint, and he wondered if things would ever be that perfect again.

Paul looked forward to the College All-Star game of 1965, in which the champion Browns would play the best collegians coming into the pro game. It was usually a fun contest, one generally dominated by the pros.

It was the first quarter when the Browns had a third and six on their own 24. Quarterback Ryan sent Paul deep and lobbed a high pass in his direction. Paul was running full speed with defensive back Paul Nelson right with him. The two went for the ball and came crashing to the ground, Nelson landing on top.

Paul didn't get up. He was taken from the field and to a hospital. He had a severe shoulder injury that required surgery. It was the start of a lost season. The injury took longer to heal then expected. Paul didn't play until the final games, catching just three passes for 30 yards.

The team repeated as champs, even with Paul sidelined, and he suited up for the championship game against Vince Lombardi's Green Bay Packers. Paul grabbed two passes in the game and played well, the injury seemingly healed, but the Pack had built themselves into football's most powerful team and were not to be denied, winning by a 23–12 count.

Now Paul's main concern was coming back. He did, and during the next three years his play elevated him to all-pro status. He grabbed 36, 32, then 50 passes, averaging more than 20 yards a catch each time. And in 1968 he had 1,067 yards to go with the 50 catches and another 12 touchdowns. And by playing three years of virtual healthy football he ended any speculation that he couldn't take the bumps of the pro grind. After his injury, some suspected he would be a fragile player, but he wasn't.

"I think I've pretty much learned the details of playing end in the past five years," Paul said. "It takes awhile to be able to adjust to certain defensive changes and run the right pattern. I don't really have a favorite pattern. I just try to make all of them look alike and run them well. Then I use the variations off them."

Coach Collier knew that better than anyone, claiming, "Paul runs the best, most precise, most detailed patterns of anyone I know."

Paul was a contented athlete. He was settled in Cleveland and raising a family there. The Browns were still a top team, making the playoffs several times, though not taking any more titles. And Paul was already thinking ahead, studying at Kent State University in the off-season, hoping to go into broadcasting when his playing days ended.

He was just as effective in 1969, catching another 42 passes for 886 yards, a 21.1 average, and 10 touchdowns. As always he didn't lead the league in numbers of catches since the Browns still had their great running game. But his average per catch and number of touchdowns were tough to beat, and that really showed the value of Paul Warfield.

The Browns whipped the Vikings in first round playoff action that year with Paul having a great day with eight catches for 99 yards. But the club came down to earth in the NFL title game, losing to Minnesota, though Paul had another four receptions and was again the best receiver on the field.

So Paul packed it in for another year. He looked forward to being with his family, studying, then preparing for 1970. But less than a month later, Paul Warfield and the fans of Cleveland received a sudden and severe shock.

Paul Warfield had been traded to the Miami Dolphins!

The news hit the sports pages like a bombshell. Fans called the team offices and local papers. Why? They all wanted to know. Why Paul?

"Other than Jim Brown he's the most exciting player this team has ever had," was the way one fan put it, and his thoughts were echoed by most others.

But the Browns had a reason. The club had quarterback problems, Ryan had retired several years earlier, and his successor, Bill Nelson, though a good signalcaller, had the worst set of knees this side of Joe Namath. The team felt it needed a young quarterback to take Nelson's place. There was a strong crop coming out of the colleges, but to get a shot at one of them the club needed a draft choice. The Dolphins had that high choice, but to get it the club had to part with Warfield. They felt it was worth the gamble. Paul was traded.

Even his teammates were shocked. Paul's receiving teammate, Gary Collins, was as surprised as anyone by the news.

"Shock," said Collins. "That's the only way I can describe it. If anybody was secure on any team throughout football, I thought Paul Warfield was. He's the best receiver in pro football."

Paul was as surprised as everyone else. He never expected to leave Cleveland or his native Ohio. Up to the moment of his trade, things had been almost too perfect for him. But he was a pro and tried to look at it that way.

"Sure, it comes as a great surprise to me," said Paul. "But this is one of the risks a professional athlete takes. I'll have to sever many wonderful relationships I've had in Cleveland."

Paul was also going from a proven winner to a team that had been born to expansion in 1966. So when Paul joined the Dolphins in the fall of 1970, the club was just in its fifth season. And in 1969, they had been dead last in their division with a 3–10–1 record. Plus 1970 would be the first year of the complete NFL-AFL merger, so the opponents would be even tougher. But the Dolphins also had a new coach in 1970, Don Shula, who had been highly successful at Baltimore. There was also a nucleus of fine players, such as quarterback Bob Griese, running backs Larry Csonka and Jim Kiick, and an improving offensive line. The defense was also toughening up, with a trade for veteran middle linebacker Nick Buoniconti giving the unit added stability.

To the surprise of everyone, Shula transformed the Dolphins into instant winners. The club finished with a 10–4 mark in 1970, second to the Colts in the AFC's Eastern Division, and they made the new playoff system as the wild card entry (the team with the best second-place record). True, the team lost to powerful Oakland, 21–14, in the first round, but they had done better than anyone expected.

As for Paul, he fit like a glove with his new team. The Dolphins were a lot like the Browns in that they relied on a ball-control running attack, and quarterback Griese didn't look for Paul all that often. But when he looked, the fleet receiver was usually open.

The two connected just 28 times their first year together, but those tosses were good for 703 yards, giving Paul a 25.1 average and six touchdowns. And to rub salt in the wound, Mike Phipps, the young quarterback the Browns drafted in exchange for Paul, sat the bench behind veteran Nelson. But Dolphin fans had absolutely no complaints about Paul Warfield.

In late October, 1971, as Paul was well into another fine season, he was accorded one of his greatest honors. There was a poll taken among the 26 NFL coaches. They were asked to pick the one wide receiver in pro ball they'd take if given a choice of all of them. The man getting the most votes by far was Paul Warfield.

Paul was flattered by the honor. When asked

again about the trade that brought him to Miami, he admitted the adjustment had been a difficult one.

"But that's over now. Since I've been with this club I've found it increasingly gratifying to work with an organization willing to work hard for a goal."

Soon it was obvious that Paul knew what he was talking about. The Dolphins were working toward a goal, and by now their story is well-known. A first place finish in 1971, then a march through the playoffs until being stopped by Dallas in the Super Bowl.

But in '72 and '73 the club played as well as any ever on the gridiron. The 1972 season was unbelievable. The Dolphins were unbeaten in the regular season, then marched through the playoffs and won the Super Bowl over Washington. In 1973, they lost twice in the regular season, yet were better than ever in the playoffs, taking a second straight Super Bowl, this time over Minnesota.

And through it all Paul Warfield remained a potent striking force. He had 43 receptions in '71, getting 996 yards, 11 touchdowns, and a great 23.2 average. In '72 he caught just 29, but still averaged almost 21 yards a catch and was the clutch man all year long. He had 29 again in '73 as the team continued to use that great running game, but 11 of those were for scores, indicating once more how he operates in the clutch. And his per-catch average was still up there, despite the new zones defenses which supposedly took away the long pass.

"No, I'm not a believer in the long pass, per se," Paul told a reporter who asked about his receiving and about zones. "The percentages are not good for the receiver or the passer in completing the long ones. If you're going to be successful at the passing game, you're going to have to make your living at the medium distance to short passes.

"There are too many factors with the long ball. You've gotta have the arm, the judgment, the protection. And even if the receiver is an Olympic sprinter, it takes nearly four seconds to run 40 yards downfield from a crouch start. No offensive line can protect for that long consistently. Plus zone defenses have taken away not only the bomb, but also some of the 15 or 20-yard passes. That's why more backs are catching the ball, but I still feel I can get free on a number of patterns."

That was for sure. Paul was settled into Miami now, a great favorite with the fans and his teammates. He also had his own radio show and a chance to prepare for a second career when his playing days were ended.

He showed there was still plenty of playing left however, when he had one of his greatest days at the end of the 1973 season, catching four touchdown passes against the Detroit Lions. As mentioned earlier, the Dolphins took a second Super

Bowl that year. But before the 1974 season started, another bombshell involving Paul hit the sports pages.

It was announced that Paul, Larry Csonka, and Jim Kiick had signed huge contracts to play with the Memphis Southmen of the new World Football League in 1975. All three players said they hated leaving the Dolphins, but wanted the long-term financial security their guaranteed contracts offered. They'd still have to play the 1974 season with Miami.

It was another good year for Miami. They took the divisional title, but this time fell short, losing to Oakland in the playoffs. None of the three players gave any less than his best. Paul had a bad hamstring injury at the beginning and missed several games, yet still finished with 27 catches for 536 yards and his usual, sparkling 19.9 per-catch average. He could still go get them.

The World Football League opened in '74 and many teams lost money. There was some question whether the league would operate again in '75. The three Dolphins were asked about this. Paul said if the league didn't operate, he'd seriously consider retiring.

"At my age you have to start asking questions. Can I perform the way I want to perform? A man has to be honest with himself. You set up certain standards and if you don't meet those standards you examine yourself to find out why. Eleven years is a long time in this league. Some days I'm tired of football, some days I'm not. The game isn't as challenging as it once was, but then again there's still something there. It's still a challenge to go out and try to beat the odds. If the WFL folds I don't know what I'll do."

But as of the summer of 1975 the WFL seems ready to try again, and Paul, Csonka, and Kiick will be headed to Memphis. And Paul Warfield will be out to show new fans the same moves that have thrilled NFL people for more than a decade.

He may not be quite as fast as he was, but he's still smooth and deadly. Paul has also taken care of himself and kept the injuries to a minimum. In fact, with the exception of the shoulder injury his second year, he has never had a crippling blow to keep him on the shelf for a long period of time.

In a way it's strange to see Paul going to Memphis. There was a time when he didn't want to even leave Ohio. But much has happened since those days. Paul Warfield is a much more secure person, an established superstar who has planned his football career well, and is planning his post-football career the same way.

So he does what is best for him, knowing he can return home when it's over, and knowing he'll come home after playing some of the best football ever seen in the National Football League. And when that happens, Paul Warfield will have earned a good rest.

Gene Washington

Gene Washington didn't become a pass receiver until his junior year in college. Three years later, the very same Gene Washington was named on almost every all-pro team in the land. And the great wide receiver of the San Francisco 49ers has been operating at that level ever since.

Of course, it's not nearly as simple as it sounds. Not everyone could make such a rapid transition from one position to another so quickly and so well. But Gene Alden Washington is a remarkable young man, in more ways than one.

Handsome, strong, bright, quick, articulate, committed, Gene has always been a leader and an achiever. In fact, before he switched to end, he was a quarterback, right through high school and into his college career at Stanford University. Why did Gene change positions in the midst of his college career? It took a big decision from a big man.

"I wasn't doing too well at quarterback," Gene said. "I didn't have to be a genius to know that since I had something like 11 interceptions in five games. The problem was I just couldn't throw that well, and I wasn't going to be a great quarterback if I couldn't throw well. I also knew that there weren't many real opportunities for blacks at quarterback in the pros. So unless I had outstanding ability I didn't stand a chance.

"Don't get me wrong. If I thought I could make it as a QB I wouldn't have changed. But I realized I had good hands and good agility and I thought I'd give it a try. I did have one advantage. As a quarterback, I always wished a receiver would do certain things. So when I switched to receiving, I tried to keep in mind how much time the quarterback has and to think of the things I wanted the receiver to do when I was passing."

What this entire explanation adds up to is the most important decision in Gene Washington's life. For a year after becoming a receiver, Gene became an all-America, catching passes thrown by big Jim Plunkett. He then moved on to the 49ers as a number one draft choice, and became a star from the first game of his rookie year.

But Gene is more than just an outstanding football player. He a concerned human being, one who has been working to help other black people since his high school days. He's also a perfectionist who looks for success in all fields, and sees himself continuing down a successful path long after his gridiron days are over.

California has been Gene's home base for a long time now, though he was born in Tuscaloosa, Alabama, on January 14, 1947. Gene and his four brothers had a happy childhood which was made even happier when Gene was seven. That's when his parents decided to move to Long Beach, California, where Mr. Washington went to work as an industrial painter for the Long Beach Naval Shipyard.

Gene loved California. The sun was usually shining so Gene and his brothers could go out and play ball anytime they wanted. Mr. Washington made a good living and the family never went hungry. At the same time, both parents always stressed the importance of education and all five Washington boys studied hard. In fact, though Gene was the most outstanding athlete in the family, his four brothers also attended colleges on athletic scholarships.

By the time Gene attended Long Beach Polytechnical High School he was nearly at his full height of 6-1, and already a rising star on the gridiron and on the basketball court. He played quarterback, of course, and was a guard on the hardwood, achieving all-city honors in both sports before he was through.

And that wasn't all he did in high school. Even with the constant pressure of two sports seasons, Gene maintained a 3.6 grade average, very close to a perfect 4.0, which was undoubtedly what he was going after.

That wasn't all. In his senior year Gene was elected Student Body President at Polytechnic. That one wasn't easy. The school was about 90 percent white, and Gene lost the first two times he ran, but he stuck with it and finally succeeded.

"My basketball coach talked me into running for sophomore president," he recalls, "and I did, but lost. Being president really didn't mean that much, but I didn't like the idea of losing. So I ran again as a junior . . . and lost again. But by my senior I was captain of the football and basketball teams, and well known at the school. So I went all out and ran a strong campaign and finally won."

That was just one example of Gene's perseverence and determination to succeed. If he had an early influence in those days it was his cousin, a man named Willie Brown, who was also a fine student-athlete.

"Willie was a great high school athlete and great college player," says Gene. "He played pro ball for the Rams and Eagles before going into coaching. He's now an assistant at USC. I kind of always wanted to do what he had done. As a youngster I never really thought about college or pro ball. I took things one step at a time. But I always had

Willie's example before me and it kept me going on to the next step."

Not too many people outside the Polytechnic campus knew about Gene's three tries for Student Body President. But plenty of people knew about his exploits on the gridiron. The team was a powerhouse Gene's junior year and he was the starting quarterback. The team was on its way to the championship when someone inadvertently broke a conference rule, the penalty being the title. The next year Gene didn't have the same kind of material to work with, but he still passed for more than 1,500 yards and ran the ball very well.

By then it was obvious that Gene was A-1 college material, a black scholar-athlete whose presence would enhance any campus. And plenty of the good ones tried to get him. There were more than 50 scholarship offers with Gene finally narrowing it down to three schools—Harvard, Princeton, and Stanford. The first two were prestigious Ivy League schools in the East. They didn't play top-flight football, but a few Ivy gridders have gone on to the pros. Their big forte was academic. With a degree from either school, Gene would be able to write his own ticket to almost anywhere.

Yet Stanford wasn't that different. Located on the west coast and a member of the Pacific Eight Conference, which included powerhouses such as USC and UCLA, Stanford played big time football. But the school also had an outstanding academic reputation. And unlike some other big time football schools, athletes were also treated as students and weren't segregated from the rest of the student body.

Add to this the fact that Gene could remain close to home and the decision was made. Gene would attend Stanford. That made many people happy, none more than football coach John Ralston.

"Gene was the number one athlete desired by Stanford," said the coach. "He will not only be a fine football player, but a good student and leader as well."

Later, Gene talked about his decision and some of the things he considered when making it.

"First of all, I really wasn't any kind of radical then and my thoughts were geared to getting into the mainstream of society. I felt I could accomplish this at Stanford more so than at the other schools. And at the same time I could still play some good football against the other Pac-Eight schools."

Gene also spoke of the pressures put on young athletes by the many recruiters who pursue the top guns.

"I had my own set of rules which I stuck with no matter what. I never let recruiters take away my study time. If they want you they'll come at your convenience, not theirs. It's also important to listen to each one with an open mind, and to get as many viewpoints as you can. That way, you should be able to distinguish good advice from poor advice. And the most important thing is not to let anyone make you feel obligated, not to them or the school they represent. It's your decision and you're life, and you're the one who'll have to live with it."

Sound thinking, but very typical of Gene Washington. He would put his own advice to work during his stay at Stanford, to make decisions relating both to football and his other activities.

Football wise, he began as a quarterback, starting for the freshman team and seeing plenty of action during his sophomore year, though he shared the position with two other signalcallers. Gene was a good college quarterback. He had the ability to lead and was a strong runner off the rollout and option play. But his passing always left something to be desired and it didn't take him long to realize it.

Gene's major at Stanford was sociology. His grades were very good, as usual, and his studies began to give him a greater concern for black people and for the ghetto community around the college campus. So Gene's overall outlook had changed. No longer was he solely interested in getting into the mainstream of society. Now he wanted to help people who could never be in that mainstream, the poor blacks who were locked in the ghetto. He and some friends began a tutoring program for black youngsters in the ghetto area of East Palo Alto, California.

Soon Gene had the program organized and had

given it a name. "Interact" was the name of the student group which Gene founded and its purpose was to promote understanding between Stanford students and the nearby minority communities.

"The problem that most young people from those areas face is motivation to stay in school," Gene said. "It was easier for me because my parents were always pretty sticky about me doing well in school. Many other kids aren't that fortunate.

"Many things have changed in the last few years. The Black community has given up on integration and is trying to find pride and strength from within. A lot of white people interpret this in the wrong way. Black people won't be second class citizens any more. We're hoping that Interact will give the people some of this pride and strength. If we can do that, we'll have succeeded in our aims."

Gene's aim on the football field was to be the best player possible. At the outset of the 1967 season Gene was set to compete for the quarterback job again, though the self-doubts about his ultimate ability were beginning to creep in. The interceptions he had thrown in the last five games of the previous season still bothered him. Then something happened to force him into a decision. It was a shoulder injury, one that further hampered his throwing. That's when Gene finally reached his fateful decision. He would be a quarterback no longer. A switch to wide receiver seemed the best logical solution.

"I looked at everything carefully," Gene said, "and the change made sense. All the athletic experience I had would help me make the change, even my basketball career in high school. That helped my hands and my quickness, my ability to change directions quickly."

The transition was rapid. By the time the 1967 season opened Gene had won himself a starting job. Though the Stanford quarterback situation was unsettled, Gene became the primary target, no matter who was doing the throwing. In his first year as a wide receiver he grabbed 48 passes for 575 yards, figures that many passcatchers couldn't match despite years of experience at the position.

Gene was a wiry, 185-pounder, quick and fast, and a lot stronger than he looked. In fact, he had an almost stiff way of moving, his back almost arched, very erect. Sometimes it looked as if a good shot would break him in half. But it didn't. Gene could take the defenders' best hits and come right back for more. And right from the beginning he had the big-play potential, the ability to catch the ball in a crowd, or when a defensive back was zeroing in on him. He never heard the footsteps, just concentrated on catching the ball.

When he returned for the 1968 season he finally had his quarterback. Big Jim Plunkett was the team's quarterback and he was ready to become one of college footballs all-time great throwers. Plunkett had a world of ability, all right, but he also had a man to catch his bullets—Gene Washington.

The two clicked right from game one, when Stanford walloped San Jose State, 68–20. Plunkett completed 10 passes for 277 yards and five of them went to Gene, who gained more than 100 of those yards himself.

Several weeks later the two made national headlines. Gene had caught 13 Plunkett passes in a single game, taking three long ones into the end zone for touchdowns. Many people had predicted that Plunkett would be more than an ordinary quarterback. But few realized that Gene Washington would become an outstanding pass receiver so very fast. But week after week he proved all over again that he was no fluke. Suddenly, NFL scouts began flocking to the Stanford games not only to watch Plunkett, but to check out Gene Washington as well.

Gene's life was taking many turns in a short period of time. During the season he also met a girl, Cynthia Watson, a beautiful girl who attended the University of Southern California. Cynthia was the USC Homecoming Queen and always had to sit in their rooting section. Cynthia's loyalty never wavered . . . except when USC played Stanford. Then she rooted for Gene. She had good reason. The two were in love and married shortly after Gene's graduation in June of 1969.

But in the meantime there was still football.

The scouts were beginning to call Gene the best receiver in college football. And John Brodie, the great quarterback of the San Francisco 49ers and a Stanford alumnus himself, was rapidly becoming Gene's number one fan.

"This kid is really amazing," said Brodie. "You put this down. Gene Washington will be a number one draft choice in the pros. He's just a natural as a receiver."

As for Gene, he admitted that the transition had been smoother and had come faster than even he anticipated.

"I always try to run very careful, precise patterns, and I can feel they're improving from week to week. But many of my moves just seem to come naturally. There may be some guys who are faster, but I can keep up with any of them in a short sprint . . . and football is a game of short sprints."

Short sprints or long, Gene did the job all season long. When it ended, Stanford had won the Pac-Eight title and was headed for the Rose Bowl. And as for Gene, he had grabbed 71 passes for 1,117 yards and eight scores. He was surely one of the top receivers in the entire country.

From there, Stanford went on to win in the Rose Bowl, with all-Americas Plunkett and Washington again performing admirably. Then Gene went to play in the East-West Shrine all-star game. Matched against the other top college receivers, he grabbed seven big passes and was named the Outstanding Offensive Player of the Game. It was now a foregone conclusion that Gene would be a very high draft choice of the pros.

That's just what happened. And Gene couldn't be happier, because the pick enabled him to remain in his beloved California. Gene became a number one pick of the San Francisco 49ers. In fact, the 49ers had two number one picks in 1969, and the other choice turned out to be all-America tight end Ted Kwalick. Forty-niner fans were ecstatic. In one quick draft, the team had practically revamped the entire receiving corps.

Picking the duo was easy, signing them was not. Both Gene and Kwalick had a preconceived idea as to their worth. They negotiated separately, but as of early June, the results were the same. Neither had signed.

In Gene's case, the initial offer was said to be about $80,000 for three years. Gene's agent termed the offer "an insult" claiming that the team was way below what other clubs were paying their top picks.

It was the old cat-and-mouse game that most clubs played with their top draftees ever since the NFL–AFL war of the early 1960's, when the price of rookies skyrocketed. In reality, the club wanted both players signed very badly, and within a week or so they agreed to terms with Gene. The contract price elevated to around the $150,000 mark. Kwalick's holdout lasted longer and, ironically, it took the tight end a lot longer to acclimate himself to the pro game.

Gene looked good almost from the very first day he was in camp. He wanted to excel very badly, though he never viewed football as the ultimate. He knew there'd be other things.

"I want a lot out of football," Gene said, "but I want a lot out of life, too. And I expect to use my football success as a stepping stone to success in other things when my career ends."

Gene already knew there were other avenues. During his holdout he did some work with comedian Bill Cosby, and the word was that Cosby was ready to offer Gene a part in his new series. But once he signed his contract, Gene was prepared to devote all his time to football.

He was joining a team that couldn't seem to build itself into a contender. There were always fine players present, but just not enough of them. Since 1965, the club had been remarkably consistent, toying with the .500 mark, checking in with records of 7–6–1, 6–6–2, 7–7, and 7–6–1. That last mark in 1968 was made under a new coach, Dick Nolan, who had hopes of rebuilding in '69. And when he saw Gene Washington operating at wide receiver, he figured one of his problems was solved.

"Gene is far ahead of the other rookie pass-catchers I've seen," said the coach. "He knows how to handle himself out there. He can do things the other rookies can't do. For instance, Jerry Levias down at Houston looks like a fine prospect, but Houston has to put him in motion to get him open. He just couldn't fight the backs downfield. Gene is different. A back can't just bump him at the line and forget him. He has the strength to get open, and once he gets the ball he can really move with it."

Gene was a starter from game one, and the veteran John Brodie loved throwing to the youngster right away. Gene gave the team the deep threat it had been lacking. He listened to advice from the veterans and worked hard at his own patterns and moves.

"Dick Witcher (the 49ers' other wide receiver) has been a great help," said Gene, midway through his rookie season. "He's constantly pointing out mistakes and showing me the fine points of the game.

"And I don't regret for a minute all those years I spent being a quarterback. I know how the quarterback thinks, what he's looking for, how much time he has to throw the ball, stuff like that. So I run my patterns figuring that in three seconds he's got to unload and I'd better be ready. And I know when a quarterback thinks he can get the ball to you. A guy running downfield may think he's open, but from the quarterback's view, he's not. All this has helped me greatly."

Unfortunately, the club was having troubles winning. When the season ended the club was at 4–8–2, a big disappointment. But Gene was everything they had hoped for. He caught 51 passes for 711 yards and three scores. And his efforts put him into the Pro Bowl, one of the few rookies ever to be chosen for that honor.

Before the 1970 season began, Gene talked about winning and about his hopes for the upcoming campaign. He had always played on winning teams and didn't like losing one bit.

"The Rams are a winning team because they expect to win," Gene said. "If they're 20 points behind with, say, eight minutes left they still know they are supposed to win and they make it happen. In college ball USC wins that way, too.

"The 49ers must learn to do this. When the personnel is about even, the winning team is the team that thinks win. In many ways we're a lot like the Rams. We have a great defense, and offensively we have everything but momentum."

Then Gene talked about pass receiving, and about the new style of bump-and-run that many NFL cornerbacks were using.

"It's much harder for a wide receiver to perform against a bump-and-run cornerman who is pressing on every play. Because a bumping cornerback destroys timing between passer and receiver. The bumps keep knocking you off stride and you may be late getting to the ball. Or you may be trying so hard to get there that you'll lose your concentration."

But Gene came into the 1970 season bigger and stronger, his weight up to 190. And he wanted to be a complete player, spending much time during training camp and pre-season working on his blocking.

"Our receivers did not do a whole lot of blocking my rookie year," Gene said. "So in training camp they got us on a two-man blocking sled every day, just like the linemen. No one had ever showed me to block before. So our line coach, Ernie Zwahlen, just kept working on the fundamentals.

"I didn't really like it much at first. Who does? I didn't want to go down and hit those guys. I wanted to catch passes. But once I learned to do it right it became fun. I got a good feeling, knocking a guy down the right way and knowing I was helping the team. Now, anytime I get a chance to go after a defensive man, I do it."

But Gene didn't forget how to catch. Brodie began throwing to him early and often in 1970, and the team began winning. Quarterback Brodie was having a fine year and gave some of the credit to the play of Gene Washington.

"Gene has a way of finding openings in the defense," said the QB. "He was good right from the start and he keeps getting better. I'd say right now he has to be the best in the business, even though he's just in his second year."

So Gene kept grabbing the passes and the 49ers kept winning. In the 13th game, against New Orleans, Gene pulled in three long passes for touchdowns and in doing so ran his yardage past the 1,000-yard mark for the year, an achievement for any receiver. And by this time Gene was often double and triple teamed, leading one coach to fault Brodie for throwing to Gene too often.

"John has so much confidence in Washington that he thinks he can just throw the ball up there and Gene will get it. But sometimes Gene has two or three defenders hanging all over him and he's just not a miracle man."

Despite the close coverage, Gene finished his second year with 53 receptions for 1,100 yards, the best in the entire NFL. He averaged 20.8 yards a catch and took the ball into the end zone on 12 occasions. It was an all-pro performance, and Gene was recognized as such, making most of the first teams. He had done better than anyone would have thought.

Better yet, the 49ers had cashed in as well, finishing at 10–3–1, and taking the NFC Western Division title. In the playoffs the club whipped Minnesota, 17–14, but then lost to Dallas, 17–10, for the NFC title. They were just a step away from the Super Bowl, but that would have to wait.

Gene was a superstar already. He had lived up to all the brightest expectations. He and Cynthia were well-known figures on the California scene, a handsome couple and one of the best dressed anywhere.

"My wife and I like to project our best image," said Gene. "I'm not talking about a false front, not that kind of thing. But we both love clothes and love each other to be smartly dressed. I like to be flashy, but discreet. I want to express my own personality. Athletes have an advantage in that they can express themselves; they aren't pigeon-holed by one particular style of dress. I guess we're lucky that way."

Then there was football. All-pro didn't give Gene a big head. The desire for improvement was still strong.

"I was happy with my year," he said, "but I don't think I've reached my limit. I made all-pro, sure, but I can still improve on my pass patterns. If you run a pattern the way it's meant to be run you should get open every time. Maybe I can beat a guy two out of three times. But I shouldn't be satisfied unless I can make it three out of three.

"Let's face something else. All-pro is based on your stats. Once you make it, it will be harder to get the same statistics. Paul Warfield may catch only 30 passes a year, but he's double covered most of the time. He's still better than many all-pro receivers."

Obviously, Gene was well aware of something that many fans don't know. You can't judge a man solely by his statistics. And if Gene didn't match his numbers of 1970, he could still be an improved player having an outstanding year.

There was little doubt that Gene was now one of the big cogs in the 49er attack and a very valuable member of the team. Quarterback Brodie couldn't praise him enough. And Coach Nolan was usually pretty close behind.

"As good as he was last year, Gene should be even better this year," said the coach. "He is a very intelligent receiver, has great hands and great speed. When he came into the league he couldn't block because he didn't know how. Now he can block better than 80 percent of the receivers.

"And he's a great team man. If you asked him to go back and return a punt, he'd do it. He's just a tough egg. He can go across the middle as well as go down the sidelines. The only thing that will slow him down is injury."

Teams facing the 49ers in 1971 all came in with the same defensive game plan. It read: Stop Gene Washington. They especially wanted to take the long bomb away. Sometimes they gave him the short ones, but whenever Gene tried to go deep, he'd have two or three defenders hanging all over him.

"I don't really mind too much," said Gene. "It's part of the game. Besides, when they drop another man off to cover me, it means someone else is open and the team can still move. That's the important thing."

In 1971, the other man was usually Ted Kwalick. The big tight end who was the co-number one pick with Gene in 1969, had been a bench warmer for two years, catching just 12 passes in that period. But suddenly, in 1971, he emerged to show his great potential once again. So whenever Brodie found Gene covered, he'd look for Kwalick and often find him.

That didn't mean Gene was having a bad year. If the defense let up on him for just a second, he could burn them. Against New England the 49ers had a three point lead in the final quarter. The Pats wanted the ball and decided to forget the double coverage on Gene. San Francisco was at its own 23 when Gene detected the switch.

"They're not doubling on me any more," he told Brodie. The quarterback was quick to respond, calling on Gene deep down the middle.

With just a single cornerback on him Gene sped down the middle. Brodie cranked and fired. At the release, Gene accelerated and got the step on the defender. He caught the ball in mid-stride and continued to a 67-yard touchdown. With one man on him he was almost unstoppable.

The same thing happened two weeks later against the Vikings. The Vikes abandoned the double coverage in close and from the six, Brodie threw over the middle to the diving Washington. Touchdown! The game winner in a 13–9 victory.

Once again the 49ers took the divisional title, this time with a 9–5 mark. Gene's stats were slightly off 1970, 46 catches for 884 yards, and four scores. But his yardage was tops in the NFC and his average gain 19.2 yards a catch. And the double coverage had loosed Kwalick for 52 catches. The club's passing game was tops.

Gene played well in the post-season as the club whipped Washington, 24–20. But in the NFC title game they came up short, losing to Dallas and its defense, 14–3. Close again, but no cigar.

The '72 season was very similar to '71 in many respects. Gene admitted that zones and double coverages had slowed him up, but with Kwalick getting close to all-pro himself, things were opening again. Steve Spurrier replaced the injured Brodie for most of the campaign and the 49ers won another divisional title . . . and lost again in the playoffs, this time to Dallas in the first round, by a close, 30–28 score.

Gene had 46 catches for the second straight year, with his yardage up slightly to 918. The big difference was in his TD catches, back up to 12. He was still an all-pro player of the first magnitude.

But as usual, Gene wasn't resting on his laurels. He was always thinking of the future. His handsome appearance and commanding personality had already brought in endorsements, TV acting spots, and many requests for appearances. Yet he continued to help poor youngsters, much as he had at Stanford. And he looked to other things.

"I find the business world quite fascinating," he said, "and I always try to know what's going on in the rest of the world. I'm still not sure what I'll do when my playing days are over. Whatever it is, I'll try to succeed. Law school is one possibility. But football is still first. I'd like to stay in the game for 10 years if it's possible."

And others continued to praise Gene as a top

receiver. Brodie said so often, "I defy any defender to contain Gene one-on-one. If he's not double-teamed I'll almost always throw to him because I know he'll be open."

One of the 49er coaches said it was concentration that made Gene so great. "He shuts out everything but catching the football. When he goes after a pass, he sees only the ball and nothing else."

And receiver coach Jim Shofner, always a big Washington fan, summed it all up.

"I've been here seven years and Gene is far and away the best wide receiver the 49ers ever had. In fact, I would have to classify him as one of the best I've ever seen in the 15 years I've been with professional football."

Unfortunately, the 49er team crumbled in 1973. The defense was aging and slipped over the line between aging and old. Plus the offense was unsteady, especially at quarterback, where Brodie was hurt and nearing the end of the line. Gene was beset by some nagging injuries and managed 37 catches for 606 yards, but only two scores. The club was 5–9 and out of the playoff picture early.

There was a bit of a comeback in '74, but only to 6–8, a distant second to the Rams. With the quarterback situation in chaos, Gene had for him a subpar year. He caught just 29 passes, yet his 21.2 yards per catch was the best in the entire NFL, proving that he still had all his speed and ability to go deep and get the ball. He's still at his peak, his only wish being that the 49ers can rebuild quickly so he has another shot at the Super Bowl.

Gene Washington has always been a man who speaks his mind. When several of the 49ers, including Kwalick, signed with the new World Football League, Gene was the first to admit he was happy for them.

"Yes, if they've bettered themselves, I'm happy," he said. "And I don't like those arguments about team loyalty. There isn't a guy on this club who was as proud of being a 49er as Ted Kwalick. But loyalty works both ways. When a team trades a player without his consent, nobody questions the team's loyalty. But when a player jumps, everyone questions the player's loyalty."

Gene, of course, has never expressed a desire to jump leagues or play elsewhere. He and his wife like it in San Francisco. And the fans there love Gene Washington. They've been watching him sprint off the line of scrimmage and haul in passes for a long time now and they plan on watching for an even longer time. Chances are he won't disappoint them.